Reading and Interpreting the Works of

WILLIAM FAULKNER

Enslow Publishing
101 W. 23rd Street
Suite 240
New York, NY 10011
USA
enslow.com

Lit Crit Guides

Reading and Interpreting the Works of WILLIAM FAULKNER

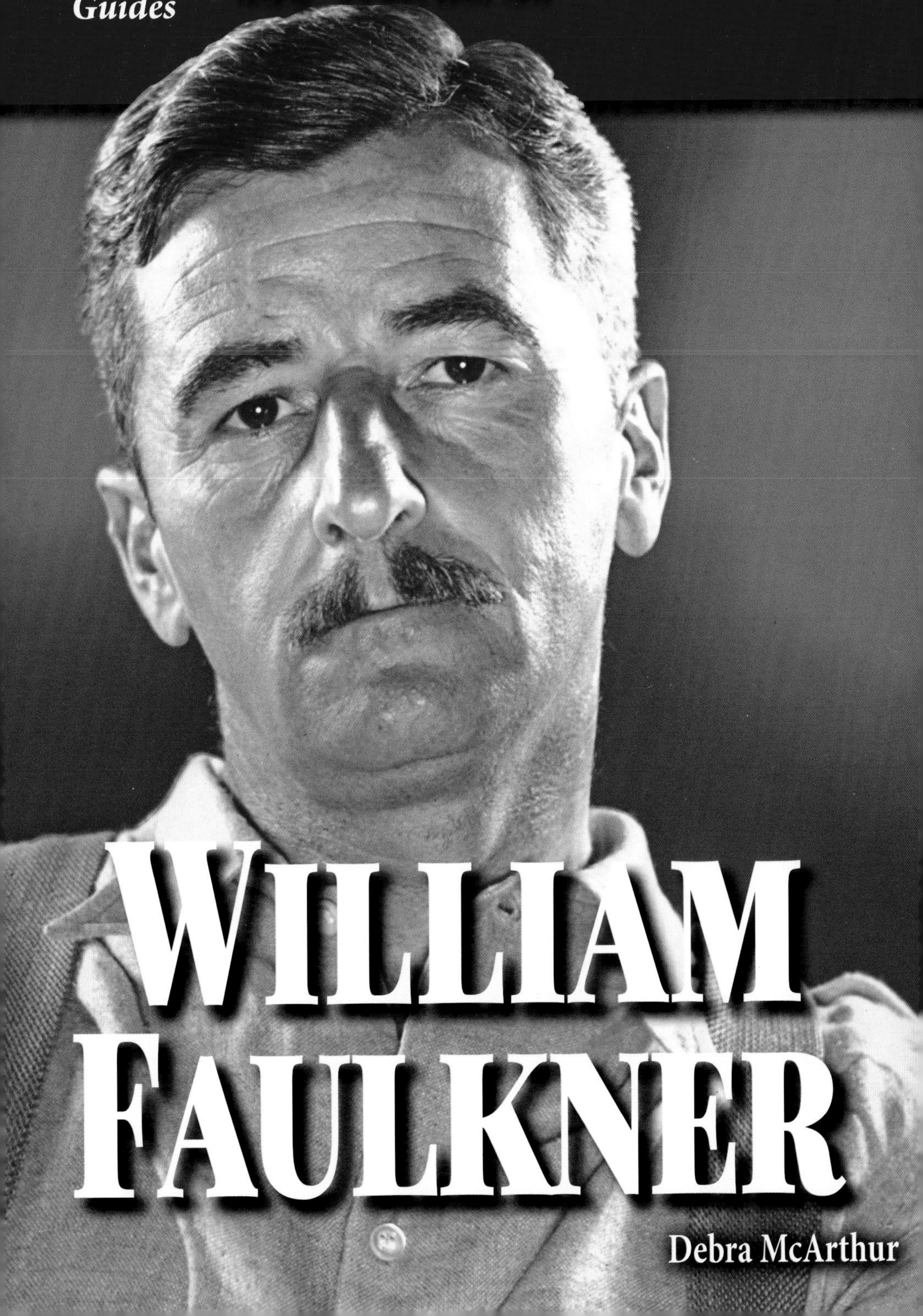

Debra McArthur

This book is dedicated to the educators who challenge themselves by teaching Faulkner's works, and to the students who accept the challenge to read and study them.

Published in 2016 by Enslow Publishing, LLC
101 W. 23rd Street, Suite 240, New York, NY 10011

Library of Congress Cataloging-in-Publication Data

McArthur, Debra.
Reading and interpreting the works of William Faulkner / Debra McArthur.
pages cm. — (Lit crit guides)
Includes bibliographical references and index.
Summary: "Describes the life and work of writer William Faulkner"— Provided by publisher.
ISBN 978-0-7660-7354-8
1. Faulkner, William, 1897–1962—Juvenile literature. 2. Faulkner, William, 1897–1962—Criticism and interpretation. 3. Novelists, American—20th century—Biography—Juvenile literature. I. Title.
PS3511.A86Z891648 2016
813'.52—dc23
[B]

2015028590

Printed in the United States of America

Portions of this book originally appeared in *Student's Guide to William Faulkner.*

Photo Credits: Cover, p. 3 Eric Schaal/The LIFE Images Collection/Getty Images; p. 6 Röhnert/ullstein bild/Getty Images; p. 10 © AP Images; p. 15 MPI/Archive Photos/Getty Images; p. 20 © age fotostock/Alamy; p. 26 AP Photo/Columbus Commercial Dispatch/Birney Imes; p. 30 © Edwin Remsburg/Alamy; p. 36 20th Century-Fox/Moviepix/Getty Images; p. 41 Universal History Archive/Universal Images Group/Getty Images; p. 46 John D. Kisch/Separate Cinema Archive/Moviepix/Getty Images; p. 52 © AP Images; p. 56 © AP Images; p. 63 © Buddy Mays/Alamy; p. 67 © Martin Norris Travel Photography/Alamy; p. 73 DEA PICTURE LIBRARY/De Agostini/Getty Images; p. 77 Harold M. Lambert/Archive Photos/Getty Images; p. 82 Hulton Archive/Getty Images; p. 86 © AP Images; p. 91 © AP Images; p. 94 © AP Images; p. 98 © AP Images; p. 104 Mario De Biasi/Mondadori Portfolio Premium/Getty Images; p. 110 Buyenlarge/Archive Photos/Getty Images; p. 116 Hulton Archive/Getty Images; p. 122 Stanley Bielecki Movie Collection/Moviepix/Getty Images; p. 128 © Gilbert Hanekroot/Alamy; p. 132 William Albert Allard/National Geographic/Getty Images; p. 137 Carl Mydans/The LIFE Picture Collection/Getty Images.

Contents

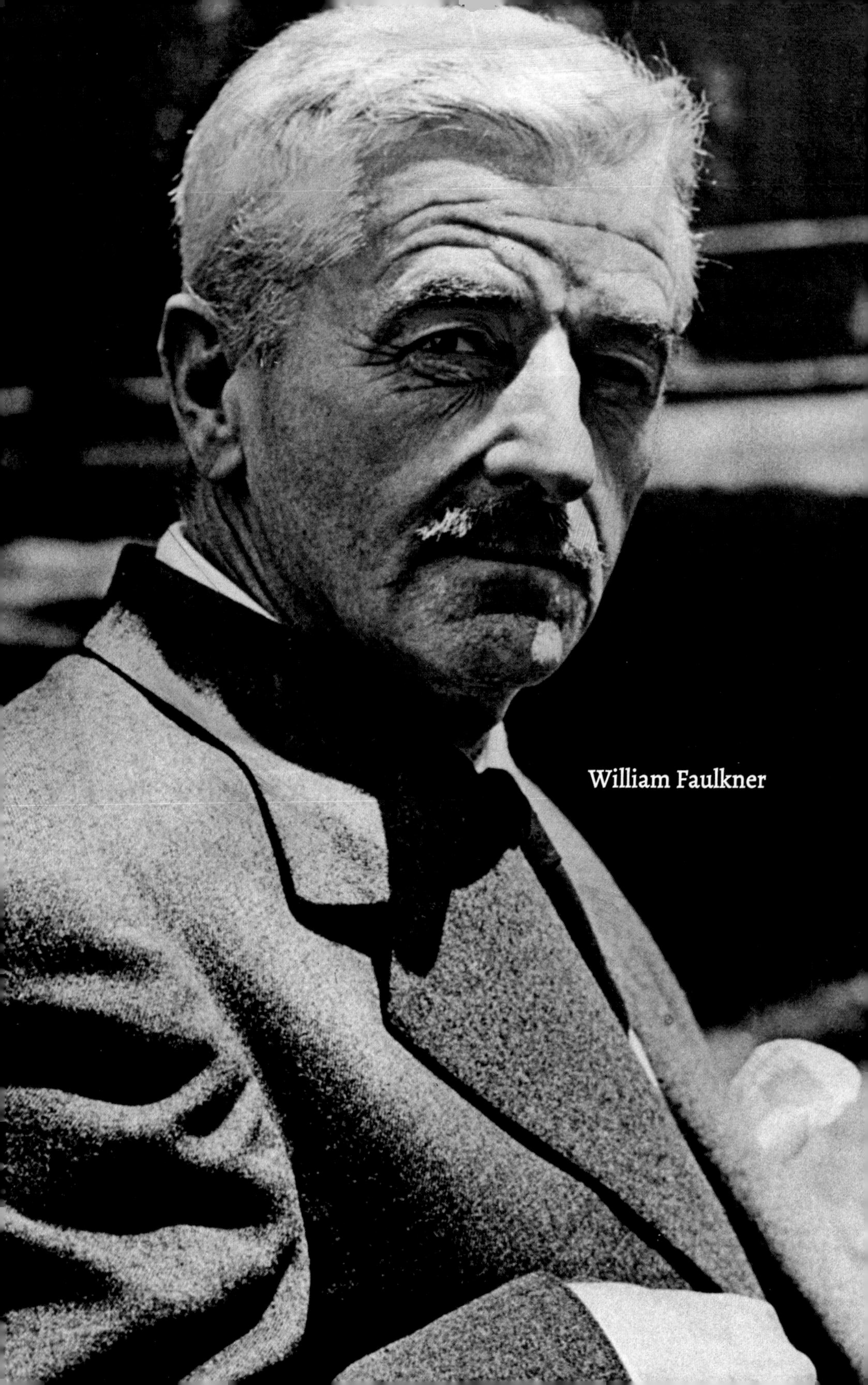
William Faulkner

1 William Faulkner's Small World

Within days of William Faulkner's death, newspapers and national magazines were eulogizing the author. An article in *Newsweek* said: "No other author in view showed promise of the supreme imaginative power by which Faulkner had created and peopled Yoknapatawpha County, the mythical arena of good and evil which America's fourth Nobel laureate in literature had added indelibly to his country's geography."[1] A tribute in *National Review* read: "Faulkner wrote for the ages . . . Yoknapatawpha did not exist before, but every literary map of the future will show just where it is."[2]

When Joseph Blotner wrote a biography of Faulkner, with whom he had become close friends through their association at the University of Virginia, he recognized that he could not take Faulkner out of Yoknapatawpha any more than he could take Yoknapatawpha out of Faulkner. "This is meant to be a biography of William Faulkner's works as well as of their creator," Blotner said, "since each element of them was in some sense a product of his total life experience."[3]

William Faulkner created the fictional world of Yoknapatawpha County and the town of Jefferson, Mississippi, within it, and he populated it with five principal families, as well as their African slaves and descendants. Between 1926 and 1962, he published nineteen novels and more than seventy-five short stories, most of them set in Yoknapatawpha.

There is little doubt that the town of Jefferson is a representation of the town of Oxford, Mississippi, where Faulkner spent almost all his life. Neither is there doubt that many of the characters are representations of the inhabitants of Oxford and the surrounding countryside. Still, readers who look at Faulkner's works as being only portraits of rural Southern life are shortchanging both the author and themselves. As author Mary Cooper Robb says:

myth

Classical story, passed down through the oral tradition that is usually accepted as fictional.

colloquial

Everyday speech that is informal and might be used in casual conversation.

> Yoknapatawpha County is imaginary, but as it furnishes the setting for book after book it attains a vivid reality . . . If this limitation of setting is an aid to reality, it also has a certain danger: that many readers will come to associate characters and situation so closely with Yoknapatawpha that they will fail to see any universal application in them and will conclude that Faulkner is a "local" writer.[4]

Even though Faulkner often limited his settings, the larger ideas he presented reach much farther.

Twentieth-Century Modernism

Although Faulkner began writing at a young age, his published literary career began shortly after World War I. It was a time of change and experimentation in literature. Many writers became interested in the work of Sigmund Freud, and they incorporated his theories of psychology into the themes of their work. As society changed with the growth of cities and industries, these also became elements in the new literary style that became known as Modernism. As Faulkner's work emerged in the literary world, he quickly was associated with this new movement.

Critics often compared William Faulkner's work to that of James Joyce, for Faulkner's use of narrative techniques like stream of consciousness, in which the story is told through a character's thoughts as he experiences the plot. Faulkner sometimes uses shifting points of view in his novels, allowing different characters to tell the story. Another break from traditional narrative form is Faulkner's use of sequence. In a Faulkner novel, chapter one may begin partway through the story, and chapter two will tell of an event that happened earlier, then shift forward to a later event, then back again.

allusion

Referring to a character, setting, or other elements of a famous story to suggest a similarity.

Yoknapatawpha

In Faulkner's mind, and in the minds of his readers, Yoknapatawpha is a very real place. Several of Faulkner's books include a map he drew to show the important places in the fictional county and where different stories take place. But the name may seem quite a mouthful. If you're having trouble reading it or saying it, here is some help. This is a YouTube video that shows a picture of the Yoknapatawpha map, with a voice-over of Faulkner spelling and saying the name:

www.youtube.com/watch?v=uE_bxElDhrk.

Faulkner works at his typewriter at his home, called Rowan Oak, in 1950.

Modernism also made use of allusion, referring to familiar stories from mythology and the Bible. For example, the novel *A Fable* uses the framework of the biblical story of the week of Christ's crucifixion to tell the story of a soldier in World War I. Faulkner uses characters named Marya and Marthe to suggest Mary and Martha from the Bible.

modernism

Literary style that originated after World War I. Techniques of modernism include use of stream-of-consciousness narration, application of psychological theory to characters, and events that are not in chronological order.

plot

The events of the story; what happens.

Faulkner often uses symbolism in his stories to hint at deeper meanings. In the opening scene of *The Sound and the Fury*, the muddy underpants of a little girl hint at the promiscuous behavior she would engage in when she became older. His frequent use of clocks and chimes in the second section of the book symbolizes the change that comes with the passage of time.

Faulkner's use of language is unique. He captures the colloquial, or everyday, language of his characters so well that their voices seem to speak directly into the reader's ear. His use of dialect has been compared to that of Mark Twain. At other times, Faulkner interrupts the action of a scene with a flashback or a description filled with vocabulary that may send even a sophisticated reader searching for a dictionary. His descriptions of nature may be filled with so much imagery as to become poetic.

These techniques can be challenging for readers, but most modernist literature was intended for educated and sophisticated audiences. Readers are sometimes frustrated by the shifting points of view, and they may find the sequence of the plot hard to follow. Faulkner scholar Edmond Volpe says, "In comparison with novels written in more traditional form, a Faulkner novel places a considerable burden on the reader . . . Faulkner's techniques may sometimes exasperate, but they are effective in compelling the reader to join in the writer's search for truth."[5]

Faulkner's Cast of Characters

Faulkner used several types of people repeatedly in his stories. Although these characters fall into several categories, not all of Faulkner's characters fit neatly into one category or another. Faulkner is seldom that easy to classify, and some characters may have characteristics from more than one category.

stream of consciousness

Style of narration in which the story is told through a character's thoughts as he or she experiences the events.

One of Faulkner's most frequent type of protagonist, or main character, is the young man moving from boyhood to manhood. This character struggles with his new role in society, accepts or rejects the traditions of his family, and experiences a range of emotions associated with his loss of innocence. He is sometimes an intellectual who struggles with the fact that these changes may not be logical. Quentin Compson in *The Sound and the Fury* is an example of this type of character, as is Lucius Priest in *The Reivers*.

Faulkner's Southern traditions make some of his characters prisoners of their society. Although they may consciously seek to break free of the expectations of others, they just cannot seem to accomplish it. Miss Emily of "A Rose for Emily" is this type of character. She is denied the chance to find a husband first by her father and then by the townspeople, who object to her desperate attempt to break free of traditions. The gruesome ending of the story reveals Emily's pathetic attempt to hold on to both love and dignity.

Another frequent Faulkner character type is the individualist. This character recognizes the traditions of his or her past but refuses to be held to them. Although breaking free of the past has great cost, the character is willing to accept the consequences. Candance Compson in *The Sound and the Fury* recognizes that her family is dying because they cannot love and are held prisoner to the traditions of the past. She breaks free of those restraints, even though she can never return to her family and can never again see the daughter she has left behind. The English runner in *A Fable* is another example of the individualist. Although the corporal who is executed for mutiny was his role model, the English runner is the character who continues to try to break the cycle of war of the past and spread the hope for peace, even though he has already been maimed and will continue to be punished.

Faulkner often draws on the antebellum, or pre–Civil War, past of the South for his characters. He frequently uses one or more characters in the role of the Southern gentleman, who embodies and perpetuates the traditions of the South. In some stories, this character is wise, kind, and a worthy mentor, respectful of both African Americans and whites. Lucius Quintus Priest, the grandfather of the protagonist in *The Reivers*, is

flashback

A story inside a story that tells about something that happened before the main story.

imagery

Use of sensory details; how things, look, smell, feel, sound, or taste.

one such character. In other stories, this character represents the worst sides of the slavery traditions. An example of this character is Lucius Quintus Carothers McCaslin, who fathered a child with his slave, then fathered a child with his own daughter.

symbolism

Using one element in a story to stand for something else.

protagonist

Main character in a story, usually the one through which readers experience the story.

Faulkner's white characters share Yoknapatawpha with their slaves before the Civil War and with the descendants of those slaves after 1865. Faulkner often uses older African American women characters as affectionate, self-sacrificing mother substitutes, such as Dilsey in *The Sound and the Fury* and Aunt Callie in *The Reivers*. Older African American men are usually kind, wise, and have keen perception, like Uncle Parsham in *The Reivers*. Many of Faulkner's African American characters, unlike many of the white characters, have a strong bond to God and to the earth. This gives them strength and peace to accept both life and death.

Faulkner does not always make it easy to get to know his characters. His style of shifting points of view and stream-of-consciousness narration require readers to use patience when they begin a book or story. Mary Cooper Robb advises that readers of Faulkner "must get into the mood they feel when they move to a new town . . . We know we do not meet and know everyone at once . . . We hear conversations that do not mean anything to us, but we find out later those few sentences have meant a great deal to someone else."[6]

The Southern tradition of slavery had a strong influence on Faulkner's writing. His portrayal of slaves was often more sympathetic than that of his white characters.

Faulkner's Frequent Themes

Although Faulkner's stories are all different from one another, there are several themes that appear often. A theme is a message about human behavior or about life or society that the writer may suggest through the problem of the characters, a repeated phrase, or the use of a symbol. It is not necessarily a moral or lesson for the reader about what people should do, but it may, instead, tell what the author intends as a "truth" about life. A story may have more than one theme.

A frequent theme in Faulkner's writing is the decay of Southern society. This theme may be suggested by a setting that includes houses that are falling down or being torn down to make way for new things. In *The Sound and the Fury*, for example, the Compsons' house falls into ruin just as the family is disintegrating.

Faulkner's characters often have strong feelings about tradition and display sadness for the passing of the grand days before the Civil War. These characters believe that in the antebellum period, stately plantations added beauty to life, and everyone knew their rightful place in the social structure and accepted their roles. Gentlemen knew the code of moral behavior, which included manners and respect for women. Women understood the importance of ladylike behavior, and virginity was sacred in a young woman. In Faulkner's stories of modern times, these values are threatened and the social order is upset.

theme

A message about human behavior or about life or society that a writer may suggest.

The issue of relations between African Americans and whites is also a frequent theme in Faulkner's work. Faulkner's pre–Civil War characters accept slavery in their society, and the best among them exhibit "gentlemanly behavior" toward their slaves, which includes humane treatment and respect. Other characters, including those in the principal families of Yoknapatawpha, abuse their slaves. The guilt that their descendants feel in the years after the Civil War (and that they will not admit) causes them to employ the descendants of slaves who previously served their families, even generations after slavery has ended.

Faulkner often uses his young male characters to illustrate a theme of initiation into the adult world. As these characters explore their own change from boyhood to manhood, this change often mirrors the idea of change in society. The young man who struggles with his own role in the adult world may also realize that the world itself has changed. The "truths" he has always accepted may be only illusions. Just as he learns the "facts of life" as they relate to sexual maturity, he may learn that the "facts of life" of his family and his society contain some dark truths that he must accept.

Often, Faulkner's young boys have grown up surrounded by African American servants that they have admired and even loved. Now, the young boy must accept his role in a white society that forbids the kind of friendly relationship he has had with them. This can create deep conflict. According to Edmund Volpe, "The boy knows that the Negro is not his inferior, but to defy that code is to alienate himself from his family, his society, and his heritage. Faulkner's hero is also deeply troubled by the guilt which his ancestors incurred in enslaving a people, a guilt which is equally his own."[7]

The use of these themes suggests a deeper meaning to Faulkner's stories than just the events in the story. What happens in a story becomes less important than why it happens and what its effects will be. Faulkner's stories explore many generations of his fictional families, and the actions of ancestors continue to have consequences on their descendants. As Volpe says: "A Faulkner novel is structured to tell a story and at the same time to explore the social, historical, and moral significance of that story."[8]

Faulkner was raised on legends: family legends, community legends. He absorbed the skills of storytelling as he sat on the steps of the courthouse in Oxford, listening to the locals tell their tales. His own family history and the stories of Civil War generals and scoundrels all combined in his memory. He practiced his art in poetry, short stories, novels, and movie screenplays. As an artist, he took those stories beyond the literal level to a symbolic level to create a body of literature that would tell more than just stories: Faulkner wanted to tell the truth. It was the truth about the South, good and bad, and the truth about man, good and bad.

2 The Young Writer

William Faulkner was born William Cuthbert Falkner in 1897. His family (with the surname spelled without the "u") had a long and respected history in Mississippi. His family lore was almost legendary in the area and was certainly legendary in the family. His great-grandfather, William Clark Falkner, was a colonel in the Confederate army during the Civil War. The family referred to him as the Old Colonel. He was a businessman, lawyer, and politician. He also wrote a best-selling novel. Family stories and regional stories were an important part of young William's life, so it seems natural that family history is a central element in much of his work. Biographer Joseph Blotner says that William Faulkner "drew more extensively on family and regional lore than any other major American writer . . ."[1] The Old Colonel's son, John Wesley Thompson Falkner, was a successful lawyer and moved his family to Oxford, Mississippi. He became deputy US district attorney for his district. He inherited the Gulf & Chicago railroad operation his father had begun. Although J. W. T. Falkner's son Murry was not interested in his classes at the University of Mississippi in Oxford, he liked working on the railroad. He held many jobs with the railroad, including fireman, engineer, and conductor.

William and his family moved to Oxford, Mississippi, in 1902. Shown here is the town square, which includes the historic Lafayette County Courthouse and a Civil War monument.

Murry Falkner's Family

On November 7, 1896, Murry married Maud Butler, and the couple moved to the town of New Albany, where Murry worked in the railroad office. When Maud gave birth to their first child on September 25, 1897, they named their baby William Cuthbert Falkner in honor of the child's great-grandfather, the Old Colonel. A year later, the Falkners moved to the town of Ripley when Murry received a promotion with the railroad. The following spring, Maud gave birth to a second son, Murry C. Falkner Jr. Then in September of 1901, the Falkners' third son, John Wesley Thompson Falkner III, was born.

Within a few months of his third son's birth, Murry Falkner was faced with a difficult situation. His father decided to sell the railroad, and Murry lost his job. In September 1902, Murry, Maud, and their three boys arrived in Oxford, Mississippi, to live in a house just a few blocks away from Murry's father and his wife, Sally. Murry was disappointed with the loss of his railroad work, and for a number of years he went from one job to another, finding little satisfaction in any of them.[2]

"I Want to Be a Writer"

Young William, sometimes called Bill or Billy by his family, was a good student in school and enjoyed drawing and writing. Whenever his teacher would ask the children what they wanted to be when they grew up, Billy Falkner would say, "I want to be a writer like my great-granddaddy."[3] He wrote so well that his fourth-grade teacher once accused Maud Falkner of doing her son's homework for him.[4]

By 1909, Murry Falkner was running a livery stable, and William spent the summer working there. He also began to join his father on fox hunts. Both horseback riding and hunting would become pursuits that Billy would enjoy the rest of his life. Over the next few years, his interest and attendance at school dropped. He began to skip school. He still loved reading and drawing, and he wrote poetry and made up stories for entertainment, but his school subjects did not interest him.

Writer in Training

Despite his lack of interest in school, William loved stories. He spent time at his father's office listening to the men tell stories. On hunting trips, he heard tales around the campfires. The old men who gathered at the courthouse in Oxford told stories about the Civil War. Young Falkner and his brothers went to the cabin of Mammy Caroline "Callie" Barr, where she told them stories about the previous generations of Falkners and about her days as a slave. At their grandfather's house, the Falkner boys heard stories about the Old Colonel. William soon developed a talent for storytelling. He got a friend to do his chores for him by telling the friend a story each day while he worked, then leaving off at an exciting point to get him to come back the next day.[5]

During the summer of 1914, William became friends with Phil Stone, whose family had been acquainted with the Falkners in Oxford. Stone was four years older than William and had just graduated from Yale. He was interested in literature and heard that William had been writing some poetry. Stone admired the poems William showed him, and so he began to mentor his young friend in his writing and in his study of literature.

First Love

William also shared a special relationship with his childhood sweetheart, Estelle Oldham. He spent many hours at her house, listening to her play the piano, showing her his poems and drawings, and just talking. As they got older, their relationship changed. Estelle was pretty and popular and came from a wealthy family. Her parents would not accept William as a suitor for their daughter because of his father's lack of success.[6]

William began the eleventh grade in the fall of 1914 but dropped out. The following fall, he began the eleventh grade again but soon quit high school for good. He worked briefly for his grandfather as a bookkeeper at the bank. He continued to write poetry and work with Phil Stone, until Stone left Oxford in the fall of 1916 to return to Yale. About that time, Falkner became friends with Ben Wasson, a student at the University of Mississippi (also called Ole Miss). Although Falkner could not take classes because of his lack of a high school diploma, he submitted drawings for the yearbook, and one of them was accepted and published in the spring of 1917.

Military Service

The year 1918 was one of change for Falkner. Estelle Oldham accepted a proposal of marriage from Cornell Franklin. World War I was raging in Europe, and Falkner tried to enlist. He was rejected because he was too short. He moved to New Haven, Connecticut, to stay with Phil Stone and took a job as a clerk for the Winchester Repeating Arms Company. His employee record showed his name misspelled as "Faulkner." While he was in Connecticut, Falkner's younger brother Murry enlisted in the Marine Corps.

Stone introduced Falkner to friends at Yale, and Falkner met several British military officers who were members of a Reserve Officer Training Corps (ROTC) unit at Yale. He adopted a British accent, changed the spelling of his name to Faulkner, and went to a Royal Air Force (RAF) recruiting station in New York. He presented false documents stating that he was born in England, along with recommendation letters written by the British ROTC officers he had known at Yale. He was accepted for pilot training with the RAF and reported for training in Toronto on July 9, 1918. The war ended on November 11, when Faulkner was still in training. It was a bitter disappointment for him.[7] Although Faulkner had never seen combat, his brother Murry was wounded in France in early November.

The "Hero" Returns Home

Faulkner returned to Oxford that December, but not before his letters detailing many adventures (all imagined) reached home. When he arrived, he wore a British officer's uniform, not the uniform of a cadet. He carried a cane and explained his apparent limp as the result of an injury sustained in a crash. Some who knew him believed that the injury had happened during combat in France. Life in Oxford was not very exciting for him. Phil Stone came from Charleston, North Carolina, to visit him, and the two of them took trips to Memphis, New Orleans, and other destinations.

College Life

Faulkner continued to write poetry under the guidance of Stone. His hard work was rewarded with the publication of "L'Après-Midi d'un Faun" (French for "The Afternoon of a Faun") in the *New Republic* magazine in the summer of 1919. Despite his lack of a high school diploma, Faulkner was able to begin studying at Ole Miss that fall when the university began a program that allowed veterans to enroll without the usual entrance requirements. Several of his poems and stories were published in the student newspaper, *The Mississippian*. He spent a year enrolled in college, but dropped out the following fall.

After Faulkner dropped out, he continued to live on campus and socialize with other students. He spent time with Ben Wasson and joined a drama group called The Marionettes. He even wrote a one-act play called *The Marionettes* for the group. He also continued to write for the student newspaper. The next fall, he went to New York, where he worked in a bookstore, but he did not stay there long.

Back at Ole Miss

Faulkner returned to Oxford in the spring of 1922, working as postmaster for the campus mail room. He spent most of his time reading through magazines that came in the mail and sharing them with his friends. He held card games in the back of the post office, and he often stayed on the job only an hour or two each day. Although he usually managed the delivery of important-looking mail, he simply threw away whatever looked like junk mail. In the Ole Miss yearbook for 1923, he was named "hardest worker" at the university, in ridicule of his poor work habits in the mail room.[8] He kept the job for nearly three years, until an investigation forced his resignation.

During his years of work in the mail room, Faulkner continued to write. He wrote for student publications at the university and also submitted a few drawings. In June 1922, the magazine *Double Dealer* published a poem of his entitled "Portrait." Phil Stone was still mentoring Faulkner with his poetry, and together they sent a collection of Faulkner's poems to a publisher, The Four Seas Company.

Four Seas would not publish the poems without payment from Faulkner, so he withdrew the manuscript. In the spring of 1924, he agreed to pay the fee. His book of poems, *The Marble*

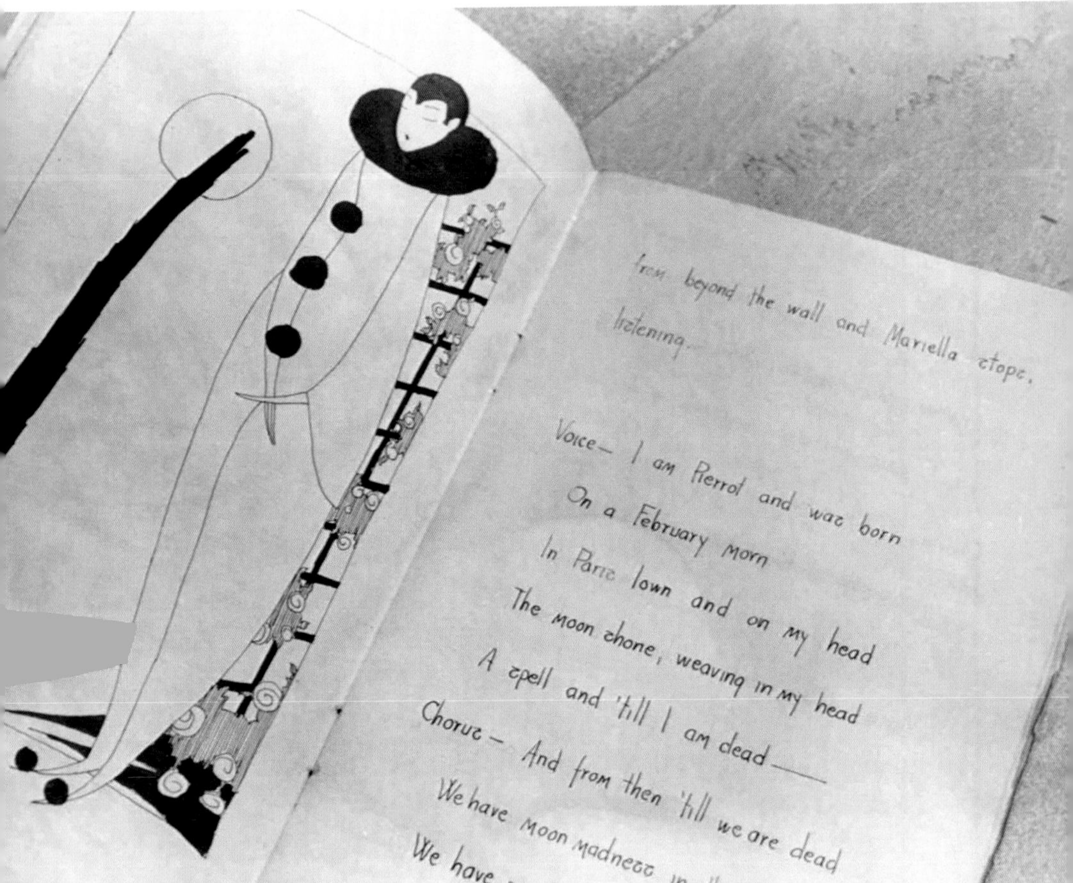

Faulkner joined the Ole Miss drama group The Marionettes and wrote a one-act play with the same name. Shown here is a copy of the manuscript of the play, handwritten and illustrated by Faulkner.

Faun, was published in December 1924. With the publication of his book, as well as the loss of his job at the university, Faulkner was ready to move on.

Community of Creativity

Faulkner planned to travel to Europe in early 1925 but went only as far as New Orleans. There he visited Elizabeth Prall, for whom he had worked at the bookstore in New York. Prall had recently married author Sherwood Anderson, and they offered Faulkner a room in their apartment.

Faulkner quickly became part of the community of writers and artists in New Orleans. He found this new environment stimulating to his creativity. He wrote poems, essays, and other pieces for the *Double Dealer* and also for the local newspaper, the New Orleans *Times-Picayune.*

Faulkner's First Novel

That winter in New Orleans, Faulkner also began writing a novel, *Mayday*, using his own experiences and those of others in World War I. The title was later changed to *Soldiers' Pay*. It is the story of a wounded fighter pilot, Donald Mahan, who returns home from the war disfigured by a head injury. The story dramatizes some of Faulkner's own disappointments, including his loss of Estelle and his inability to serve in combat in the war. Sherwood Anderson recommended the book to publisher Horace Liveright, who accepted the novel and sent Faulkner a two-hundred-dollar advance.[9]

The money allowed Faulkner to take the trip he had been planning for months. On July 7, 1925, he left New Orleans. He landed in Genoa, Italy, on August 2, then spent the next four months traveling in Italy, Luxembourg, France, and England. During his time in France, he worked on a novel he titled *Elmer*, a book he never finished. On December 2, he boarded a ship bound for New York. He was back in Oxford for Christmas, but he returned to New Orleans in February, in time for the release of *Soldiers' Pay*. Reviews for the book were generally good, although a few commented that the young writer lacked discipline. John McClure of the *Times-Picayune* called *Soldiers' Pay* the "most noteworthy first novel of the year."[10]

Love and Writing

After his novel was released, Faulkner continued to write, but he was back at the craft of poetry. The previous June, he had begun a relationship with Helen Baird when the two were on vacation in Pascagoula, Mississippi. At that time, he began writing a collection of poems entitled *Helen: A Courtship*. Helen's mother did not consider Faulkner a suitable match for her daughter and took her away to Europe.[11] In June 1926, Faulkner returned to Pascagoula to finish the collection of poems. He dedicated the book to Helen, but she was now engaged to marry someone else.

After Helen's rejection, Faulkner began work on a new novel. In it, a group of writers, artists, and others take a yacht trip on Lake Pontchartrain near New Orleans. They engage in discussions of art and poetry, and even the relationship between an artist's work and his or her sexual self. By September, Faulkner had finished the manuscript, and Horace Liveright agreed to publish the book, now entitled *Mosquitoes*.

With the novel finished, Faulkner returned to New Orleans to collaborate with his friend William Spratling on a book they called *Sherwood Anderson and Other Famous Creoles*. Spratling created drawings and caricatures of Anderson and others, and Faulkner wrote an introduction in a style that imitated

Anderson. The book was published in December 1926, and Faulkner left New Orleans to return to Oxford. This trip to Oxford, like others in the previous year, included time spent with Estelle Franklin, who by now had two young children and a marriage that was falling apart.

"Father Abraham" and Yoknapatawpha

During that winter, Faulkner began a story he called "Father Abraham." In it, he created the histories of the Snopes and Sartoris families of the northern Mississippi area of Yocona County, which he later named Yoknapatawpha County. Faulkner drew on the family stories he had heard of his ancestors and also worked in a history of the Civil War and Reconstruction. His characters were based on people from his hometown.

Eventually, these stories became the basis for a novel he called *Flags in the Dust*. This work laid the foundation for the writing he would produce for many years to come. According to literary critic Martin Kreiswirth, "The characterization in *Flags in the Dust* points toward much of Faulkner's future work. Almost every major figure in the novel reappears in some form or other in subsequent texts . . ."[12]

Faulkner finished the novel in September 1927, and he sent it to Liveright with an enthusiastic letter announcing it as the "best book you'll look at this year."[13] At the end of November, Liveright wrote to Faulkner, rejecting the book. He told the author: "My chief objection is that you don't seem to have any story to tell. . . ."[14] Martin Kreisworth says the real problem with *Flags in the Dust* is that Faulkner attempted to tell too many stories. He believes that *Flags in the Dust* "focused on too many families, introduced too many characters, offered

Faulkner wrote his first novel, *Soldiers' Pay,* while he was living in this house in New Orleans.

too many lines of action, and provided too much descriptive detail."[15]

Turning Rejection into Success

Faulkner was disappointed by the rejection, and he even threatened to "sell my typewriter and go to work."[16] Instead, he returned to the stories in "Father Abraham" to develop more material. In the meantime, he decided to send *Flags in the Dust* to a different publisher. His old friend from college, Ben Wasson, was now working for a publisher in New York, so Faulkner sent *Flags in the Dust* to him in February 1928.

For his next book, Faulkner drew on the same world he had created for *Flags in the Dust*, but now he focused his attention on a different family, the Compsons. He narrowed his focus to concentrate on the family relationships and the individual personalities of a smaller cast of characters. This new novel energized him, and he finished the manuscript in about five months. He claimed that he wrote the book *The Sound and the Fury* with no expectation of publishing it. Just as he finished *The Sound and the Fury*, he had good news from Ben Wasson: The publisher Harcourt Brace had accepted *Flags in the Dust* for publication, although they asked Faulkner to edit the book and shorten it. Faulkner went to stay with Wasson in New York, and together they worked on *Flags in the Dust*, which would be published with the title *Sartoris*.

Biographer David Minter says that Liveright's rejection of *Flags in the Dust* was an important step in Faulkner's development as a writer. "Had *Flags in the Dust* been accepted and published immediately," says Minter, "Faulkner probably would not have returned to 'Father Abraham,' and almost certainly would not have done what he did, which was to write *The Sound and the Fury*."[17]

Soldiers' Pay received fairly good reviews when it was released, but it never sold very well. *Mosquitoes* received mixed reviews, but it was not as well received as *Soldiers' Pay*. When *Sartoris* was published in early 1929, many readers and critics still did not know the name William Faulkner. The book attracted little notice, and most of the reviews were lukewarm at best. A reviewer for the *New York Times* called *Sartoris* "[a] work of uneven texture, confused sentiment, and loose articulation." Some, however, recognized the potential of this new author. Herschel Brickell, writing in the *New York Herald-Tribune*, called Faulkner "a novelist of real imaginative power, who is more than half a poet."[18]

3

Faulkner's Breakthrough: *The Sound and the Fury*

The year 1929 was a turning point for Faulkner in his professional career. *Sartoris* was published in January, and Faulkner offered *The Sound and the Fury* to Horace Liveright and then to Alfred Harcourt. Neither accepted the book for publication, but in mid-February, the new publishing company of Jonathan Cape and Harrison Smith agreed to publish it. With three novels now published and the fourth accepted, Faulkner's discouragement and his intention to "sell his typewriter" were forgotten.

Although *The Sound and the Fury* was Faulkner's fourth published novel, most critics consider it his first major work. When it was released near the end of 1929, critics took notice. Basil Davenport, writing in the *Saturday Review of Literature*, said of Faulkner, "This is a man to watch."[1] Lyle Saxon of the *New York Herald-Tribune* said, "I believe, simply and sincerely that this is a great book."[2] Dr. Cheryl Lester, English professor, says the book "marks the conclusion of the author's apprenticeship and the beginning of the so-called Major period of his literary career."[3]

A Family in Decline

The Sound and the Fury is the story of the decay of an aristocratic Southern family, the Compsons of Jefferson

FAULKNER'S FINEST FAILURE

Faulkner himself referred to *The Sound and the Fury* many years later as "the book I feel tenderest towards," even though it was "the book which took the most agony."[4] In 1955 Faulkner told a group of students in Japan that, in writing, "failure to me is the best. To try something you can't do, because it's too much [to hope for], but still try it and fail, then try it again. That to me is success." In this context, he said, "The finest failure was *The Sound and the Fury*."[5]

in Yoknapatawpha County. The father of the family, Jason Compson III, is descended from a line of men whose stories stretch back to before the American Revolution and include the Old Governor and a Civil War general. Faulkner's 1946 appendix describes Jason Compson III's grandfather, Jason Lycurgus Compson, as "the last Compson who would not fail at everything he touched," thus explaining Jason III's own lack of success.[6]

Jason III and his wife, Caroline, have four children, but Mrs. Compson is self-centered and shows little affection for her daughter and three sons. Compson works as a lawyer, but he is always worried about money, and the house is deteriorating around him and his family. He appears to be a caring and responsible parent at the beginning of the story, but both he and his wife are ineffectual and leave the raising of the children to their servant, Dilsey. By 1910 Compson has become cynical in his view of life and uses alcohol to escape.

By the end of the story, it is clear that the family will not continue past the current generation. The oldest son, Quentin, commits suicide. The middle son, Jason IV, is too selfish to marry and share his life (and money) with children. The youngest son, Benjamin, known as Benjy, is mentally handicapped and is castrated and later sent to an asylum. Daughter Caddy marries but is pregnant by another man and so disgraces the family. The remaining family members refuse to ever speak her name, although they accept Caddy's daughter, named Quentin after her dead uncle. When Miss Quentin grows to be a teenager, she runs away with a man from the traveling circus, presumably never to return.

The only enduring members of the household are the servants, led by their matriarch, Dilsey, descended from the slaves of the earlier generations of Compsons. Near the end of the story, Dilsey seems to be the only one who can see the missing element that causes the death of the Compson family, the reason for the endurance of her own family: love.

Various Voices

Faulkner tells most of the story through the voices of three different characters, using stream-of-consciousness narration that follows a character's thoughts wherever they go. Sometimes memories interrupt the present action, and the character's thoughts may flow in fragments of ideas. In the fourth section, Faulkner uses his author's voice from outside the story, an omniscient voice, but focuses on the viewpoints of Jason and Dilsey. The four sections cover many of the same incidents of the story but from the different viewpoints of the separate characters.

The stream-of-consciousness technique makes the first two sections of the book difficult to follow. Without any background information, the reader has only Benjy's and Quentin's disjointed consciousness through which to understand the story. This can be both confusing and frustrating. In 1946 Faulkner wrote an appendix that appeared with the book

The Sound and the Fury was Faulkner's first novel to receive widespread critical acclaim. This scene from the 1959 film version shows Jason Compson (played by Yul Brynner) as the neglectful father to daughter Caddy (Margaret Leighton).

in some later editions. The appendix gives details about the background of the family and the characters that a reader will find helpful in making sense of the book.

Benjamin's section is filled with sensory images, the things that the thirty-three-year-old man sees, hears, smells, and feels. The sensory experiences in the present (1928) cause his mind to jump to memories of earlier years. The center of Benjy's world is his sister, Caddy, who is a substitute for the mother who spends her time in her room, presumably too ill to care for her children. Caddy's growth into womanhood represents the ultimate loss for him. Long after she has left, the voices of golfers shouting "caddie" cause Benjy to bellow in grief.

To help readers recognize the shifts in the sequence of events, Faulkner wanted the original printing of the book to have the sections printed in different colors of ink. The cost of printing was too high for his publisher, however, so the edition was printed with only italics to show the beginning of sections where the scene shifts to a different time.

The second section is almost as hard to follow. Quentin is an intelligent young man, a student at Harvard, but he is in an emotional crisis. He is obsessed with his sister's loss of innocence, her marriage, and her departure from the family. His confusion leads him to confess and perhaps believe that he has committed incest with her, even though he has not. His section of the book consists of his thoughts and memories on the day he has decided to commit suicide, June 2, 1910. Like Benjy, his thoughts are a combination of events in the present and memories from the past.

omniscient narrator

A voice telling the story that is all-knowing.

The third section of the book is narrated by Quentin's younger brother, Jason IV. In 1928 Jason is the head of the household, now that Caddy is gone, Quentin is dead, and their father also has died. Jason works at the local hardware store, but he hates the job and is insulting to his employer and the customers. Like his brothers, Jason also suffered a loss when Caddy left the family. Caddy's husband had promised Jason a job in his bank. When their marriage ended, Jason lost that opportunity and the prestige and income it would have provided.

Jason takes care of his mother, but he is also stealing money from her. He provides a home for Caddy's teenage daughter, but for years he has been stealing the money Caddy sends for her daughter. Faulkner once said that Jason "represented complete evil. He's the most vicious character in my opinion I ever thought of."[7] Interestingly, Faulkner's appendix describes Jason as "the first sane Compson" since before their ancestors left Scotland and, because he had no children, "hence the last."[8]

The final section of the story is told by a voice from outside the story, and it follows Dilsey, the old servant of the Compson family. Near the end of the book, Dilsey attends an Easter church service with her family and Benjy. That morning, the Compsons have discovered that Miss Quentin, the only member of the last generation of the Compsons, has run away. As the preacher describes ". . . de darkness en de death everlasting upon de generations," Dilsey begins to cry. She continues to cry as they leave the church and tells her daughter, "I seed de beginning, en now I sees de endin."[9]

When speaking of his creation of *The Sound and the Fury* Faulkner claimed that this structure grew out of his need to tell the story. He said that he began with the idea of writing a short story about children who were made to leave their house during their grandmother's funeral. As the story of those children and their family took shape in his mind, he searched for the right way to tell it. He took the title of the book from Shakespeare's play *Macbeth*:

> Life's but a walking shadow, a poor player
> That struts and frets his hour upon the stage
> And then is heard no more; it is a tale
> Told by an idiot, full of sound and fury,
> Signifying nothing.[10]

This view of life, as little more than temporary tragedy, is the viewpoint of many of the characters in *The Sound and the Fury*. Faulkner began with the idea of his story being "told by an idiot," but could not fully tell the story that way. In a published interview, he described his narrative process this way:

I had already begun to tell it through the eyes of the idiot child . . . I saw that I had not told the story that time. I tried to tell it again, the same story through the eyes of another brother. That was still not it. I told it for the third time through the eyes of the third brother. That was still not it. I tried to gather the pieces together and fill in the gaps by making myself the spokesman. It was still not complete, not until fifteen years after the book was published when I wrote as an appendix to another book the final effort to get the story told and off my mind so that I myself could have some peace from it.[11]

Interpreting *The Sound and the Fury*

The Sound and the Fury is a complex novel. It contains many elements worthy of discussion and that suggest various ways to interpret the book. Despite the differing ways to get at the meaning, there are several messages within the book that are clear. *The Sound and the Fury* is a story of death and life and acceptance of change. There are many deaths in the novel, beginning with the death of Damuddy, the children's grandmother. Other characters who die include Quentin, Mr. Compson, and Dilsey's husband Roskus. Death is also suggested in many other images, such as the corpse of the horse in the pasture that has been devoured by buzzards. In addition, Benjy's only treasure is his "graveyard" of bottles.

End of a Culture

Faulkner lived during a time of great change in the culture of the American South. He was born in the 1800s and grew up hearing the stories of the heroes in the Falkner family, such as his great-grandfather, the Old Colonel, who fought in the Civil War. These stories glorified the "Old South" of the pre–Civil War era, when "gentlemen" owned plantations with stately houses, large plots of land, and slaves.

The time period in which Faulkner wrote *The Sound and the Fury* was one of prosperity in the North just before the stock market crash and the Depression, but it was one of deterioration in the South. The old people who remembered the time before the Civil War were dying, and automobiles were replacing the simple horse-drawn buggies and wagons.

Quentin is obsessed with preserving the traditions of Southern aristocracy. Women are expected to remain pure until marriage and be modest and ladylike, and men are expected to treat them with respect. Caddy's loss of her virginity and her promiscuity disturb him because they upset this tradition. He is also disturbed by the attitudes of Dalton Ames and Gerald Bland, who treat women only as sex objects. Quentin considers his father to be the family's keeper of these traditions, so when his father discounts the importance of virginity and honor, Quentin feels the loss even more. This "death" of Southern traditions is so serious for Quentin that

In the early 1900s, many Southerners were nostalgic for the pre-Civil War days when plantations flourished and slaves worked in the fields.

it takes away the most basic principles of life for him, and his only solution is death.

Inability to Accept Change

The theme of death is also shown through the characters' resistance to change in the book. Because life is a constant series of changes, including changes from childhood to adulthood, the denial of change must result in death. Life is marked by the passage of time, and time is also central to the novel.

The character most resistant to change is Benjy. Because of his mental defect, Benjy is stuck in childhood forever. Time has no real meaning for him; each day's events bring up memories of the past into his present consciousness. The one thing Benjy wants most is consistency, but he is denied this. He was named Maury at birth, after his mother's brother, but when she realizes his mental disability, she insists that his name be changed. This is one of the scenes from his childhood that Benjy remembers most. His castration, an obvious physical change to his body, is another. Benjy also resists change in other ways. He wants to take the same route every time he rides in the carriage to the cemetery. When Luster takes the carriage to the left side of the monument in the town square, Benjy bellows his outrage and reveals his confusion.

The change that affects Benjy most is the loss of Caddy. In her childhood, Caddy smells like trees. When she begins to mature, she wears perfume. This new smell frightens Benjy. He pushes her into the bathroom to wash off the smell. Her interest in boys and her sexual maturation ultimately take her away from him. Unlike the perfume, Caddy cannot just wash this away. She will never smell like trees again. When Caddy marries and leaves home, Benjy continues to search for her. He waits by the gate for her to come home from school; he bellows for her when he hears the golfers call "caddie." Because Benjy has no concept of time, he continues to have hope that Caddy will return.

Quentin also clings to the memory of his days with Caddy in childhood, a time when they shared a close relationship without sexual implications. As they experience puberty and an awakening of their sexual adulthood, Caddy and Quentin's connection is threatened. In Quentin's mind, his sister's sin separates them, but the sin of incest or the sin of shared suicide could bring them back together. Caddy's marriage makes both of these impossible. Like Benjy, Quentin mourns the loss of his sister.

Quentin's resistance to change is also reflected in his obsession with time. He tries to deny time by breaking the hands off his watch, but the watch still ticks. Time advances, but Quentin, with a broken watch, does not know what time it is. He goes into a jeweler's shop, not to find out the time from the many clocks inside, but to have the jeweler assure him that none of the clocks are right. At the end of the day, Quentin returns to his room at Harvard. His mind continues to race as he cleans his vest, brushes his teeth, and prepares to take his letter to the post office. Behind these actions and his unorganized thoughts, the clock continues to chime and mark the passing hours. Quentin cannot stop change any more than he can stop time. His only escape from both is death.

For Jason, the loss of Caddy brought him to his current state of misery. His loss of the promised job in the bank is a source of bitterness. He feels cheated by his sister and by his dead brother and father, left to care for his hypochondriac mother, his idiot brother, and his sister's illegitimate child. His job at the hardware store will never make him the kind of wealth he wants. The house is crumbling in disrepair, and his best attempts to make money by investing in stocks have only resulted in losses. His response is to steal money from both his mother and his niece, rationalizing that he deserves it for all the misery he endures.

Jason denies that people and things can change. He is convinced that everyone is against him. Likewise, he believes that women will never change. The first line in his narrative is "Once a bitch always a bitch." He is convinced that his niece has the "bad blood" of her mother and so is destined to be a promiscuous girl. Of course, Jason has the same personality in adulthood that he had in childhood. Jason's obsession with money is foreshadowed in his childhood by his habit of always having his hands in his pockets. Dilsey's son Versh says, "Jason going to be a rich man. He holding his money all the time."[12] At the end of the book, Miss Quentin's escape will bring an end to the money Caddy was sending, as well as the loss of the money Jason had been stealing all these years.

Jason's concept of time is less obvious than Benjy's and Quentin's, but it does fit his character. He complains about Miss Quentin being late to school, Caddy's check arriving late, and being late to his own job. As he goes through the day of April 6, he reports the time of just about every event of the day. Critic Perrin Lowry points out that Jason spends much of his time rushing around but always seems to arrive too late. When he chases Miss Quentin and the man with the bow tie, they drive off just before he can catch them. The telegram informing him of the drop in Jason's stocks could not reach him because he was chasing Miss Quentin all over town. Jason writes a message to send to his stockbroker but is told "Market closed an hour ago."[13] According to Lowry: "Jason's view of time is consistent with his general mental attitude. His dominant faculty is reason, but because his reason is never tempered by sensation or emotion, he always comes to the wrong conclusion."[14]

Only Dilsey seems to have appropriate responses to change and to time. Dilsey and her family accept death as a natural course of life. In their house they "moan" (mourn), and then go on with life. Her children are about the same ages as the Compson children, but Dilsey's children understand death. When Damuddy dies, the Compson children are kept away from the house and not told what is happening. The children think there is a party at the house. Caddy thinks that a band is going to come to play music for the party, but Dilsey's daughter Frony tells her, "They aint going to have no band . . . I knows what I knows."[15]

Dilsey sees time for what it is: the natural flow of life. She celebrates Benjy's thirty-third birthday with a cake with thirty-three candles, even though his own mother and brother will not acknowledge the occasion. She sees true time, even when the Compsons deny it. The clock in the Compson kitchen where Dilsey works on Easter morning strikes five times. "Eight oclock," Dilsey says.[16]

Caddy and Dilsey

The only Compson child who does not narrate a section of the story is Candance, or Caddy. Even though Caddy is central to the novel, she never appears in present action, only in the memories of other characters. Critic Olga Vickery believes that Caddy's loss of her virginity is the central event of the novel. "This is evident," says Vickery, "in the fact that the sequence of events is not caused by her act—which could be responded to in very different ways—but by the significance which each of her brothers actually attributes to it."[17] Caddy's sin represents loss for each of her brothers. Benjy loses the only person in

In *The Sound and the Fury,* Faulkner portrays Dilsey, the black servant, as the sole voice of reason and morality. (The character is seen here in the 1959 film version, played by Ethel Waters.)

his family who really loved him. Quentin loses the symbol of pure Southern womanhood. Jason loses his dream of wealth and advancement.

In another way, Caddy can be considered a symbol of life in this story that seems to emphasize death. The passage from *Macbeth* seems to suggest that life is little more than a shadow or illusion, and it "signifies nothing," a very pessimistic view. On the contrary, though, the final section of the book leads us to a different conclusion. In fact, in the midst of the death of the Compson family is Caddy, whose personality suggests love and life. She recognizes the dying family around her and escapes. In doing so, she leaves the rest to die. Caddy's legacy for the family is her baby daughter, again, a symbol of life. In this dying family, Miss Quentin is the only hope they have of continuing the line of Compsons past the current generation. She is denied affection from her family, and she seeks love in the only way she can—as sexual encounters. When she follows her mother's example and escapes from this dying family, she also seeks life. In doing so, she leaves the rest of them to the death they deserve—and even seem to desire.

Critic Edmond Volpe describes *The Sound and the Fury* as a "masterpiece" with an "oppressive mood of despair."[18] He points out that, despite the somber tone of the book, Faulkner's overall message in the book is a positive one. The downfall of the Compson family is the pride and selfishness that replace the love they should feel for one another. In contrast to the Compsons, the love, humility, and compassion of Dilsey will ensure that her family will endure. Dilsey's faith and compassion is most vividly demonstrated in the church service on Easter morning in the last section of the book. As Volpe says, "Dilsey is the symbol of resurrection and life."[19]

4 Triumph and Trouble

In addition to his professional successes in 1929, Faulkner also looked forward to a major personal event: his marriage to the soon-to-be-divorced Estelle Franklin. But this brought new pressure for him. Even with the recent success of his work, his income was not steady. He worried that he would not be able to support Estelle and her two children. He needed a best seller, and he needed it right away.

His solution was to write a book that would appeal to the basest of human instincts: greed, lust, and corruption. It might not be "art," but it would surely sell books. He set to work feverishly, and in just a few weeks, he was finished. The book's title was *Sanctuary.*

Faulkner again uses the setting of Yoknapatawpha County and sets the story in the town of Jefferson. His characters are corrupt politicians, gamblers, bootleggers, prostitutes, and gangsters. Into the midst of this world he brings a young girl, Temple Drake. Temple is kidnapped and brutally raped by a depraved gangster named Popeye. She is corrupted by him and becomes a willing sexual partner with another man so that Popeye can watch. Later, she helps convict an innocent man of a murder that Popeye committed. With its violence and sex, *Sanctuary* was shocking, even to Faulkner's editor. "I can't publish this," Hal Smith wrote Faulkner. "We'd both be in jail."[1]

In June, Estelle Oldham Franklin and Faulkner were married. They honeymooned in Pascagoula, Mississippi, and Faulkner spent some of the time on that trip working on *The Sound and the Fury* to get it ready for publication. Estelle and her children moved with Faulkner into a boardinghouse in Oxford. *The Sound and the Fury* was released on October 7, 1929, but it was not a financial success. Although the reviews were good, sales were not. The disappointing sales were not solely a reflection of lack of interest, though. On October 29, the stock market crashed. Once the Great Depression hit, most Americans had little money to spare for buying books.

Faulkner's Easiest Book

Faulkner took a night job at Ole Miss in the power plant. During his shift, he spent several hours each night writing. He wrote his next novel, *As I Lay Dying*, in a period of just six weeks, between late October and early December.[2] Faulkner commented on several occasions that *As I Lay Dying* was the easiest book he ever wrote. In an interview in 1955, he said, "It just came all of a piece with no work on my part. Just came like that. I thought of all the natural catastrophes that could happen to a family and let them all happen."[3]

As I Lay Dying is the story of the Bundrens, a poor family from rural Yoknapatawpha County. On her deathbed, Addie Bundren makes her husband, Anse, promise to take her back to her hometown of Jefferson to bury her. The family travels with Addie in her coffin on the back of the wagon, as buzzards circle overhead. Faulkner tells the story through the voices and different viewpoints of the characters in the book. Each of the five children responds differently to the situation, from the dutiful son who builds his mother's coffin, to the youngest, who, fearing that his mother cannot breathe in the coffin, drills holes through the top of it and into her face. The corpse and coffin survive being washed out of the wagon as they cross a flooded stream, a fire set by son Darl, and the stares and disgust of townspeople as the smell of the corpse intensifies. Dewey Dell, the only Bundren daughter, spends the journey seeking a remedy for her secret pregnancy. The varying voices and motivations of the characters tie the story together to create what Faulkner often called his "*tour de force*" [brilliant feat].[4]

Despite the onset of the Great Depression, 1930 would be a year of great productivity for Faulkner. *As I Lay Dying* would be published this year, and *Soldiers' Pay* would be published in England, but Faulkner was still not making much money from his novels. He began to write short stories because he could turn them out quickly and the national magazines paid well for them. Although he had rejections on his early stories, he was willing to revise them, and soon he began to sell them to magazines such as *Forbes* and the *Saturday Evening Post*. At this point, the characters of Yoknapatawpha County found their way into Faulkner's short stories.

As I Lay Dying was published in October, and Faulkner continued to work on short stories for the magazine market. In November of 1930, he was surprised by a box from his editor Hal Smith. It contained a printer's copy of the novel *Sanctuary*. Smith had changed his mind and decided to publish the book, but now Faulkner had second thoughts about it. He had written the book only to make money, and now he thought that it was "badly written . . . cheaply approached."[5] He wrote to Smith to withdraw the book, but Smith still wanted to publish it, so Faulkner rewrote the book and sent it back in December.

Also in 1930, the Faulkners moved into an old house that had neither electricity nor plumbing. Faulkner named the

For a time, Faulkner's life in Oxford centered around the University of Mississippi, or Ole Miss (seen here). He studied and worked at the school on and off for several years.

house Rowan Oak, after a Scottish tree by the same name that symbolized peace and safety.[6] He and Estelle also prepared for the birth of their first child.

On January 11, 1931, Estelle gave birth to a daughter whom they named Alabama. The child was born nearly two months early and survived for only nine days. The baby's death deeply affected Faulkner. While Estelle was still recovering from the birth, he made the funeral arrangements and buried the child near relatives in St. Peter's Cemetery in Oxford.

International Recognition

In February 1931, *Sanctuary* was released. Faulkner had removed some of the most objectionable material from the book, but it still contained many scenes that some critics blasted for their brutality and strong sexual content. Many readers in the South were offended by the book. Faulkner's neighbors in Oxford were ashamed, and some who purchased the book from the local drugstore had it wrapped in brown paper before taking it out of the store.[7] Despite the controversy, in the first three weeks after its release, 3,519 copies of *Sanctuary* had been sold, almost equal to the sales of *The Sound and the Fury* and *As I Lay Dying* combined. By the first of April, sales had reached 6,457.[8]

The popular success of *Sanctuary* brought more attention to Faulkner's short stories, and he sold several to magazines that had previously rejected his work. In May, he signed a contract for publication of a collection of his stories called *These 13*. Also in the spring of 1931, Faulkner received a letter from Maurice Coindreau, a professor at Princeton University, who wanted to translate Faulkner's stories into French. Coindreau began with "A Rose for Emily," but he also wanted to translate *The Sound and the Fury*, *As I Lay Dying*, and *Sanctuary*. Coindreau's work would bring Faulkner recognition overseas.

Stress and Alcohol

By this time, Faulkner was working on a new project. He took some material from two unfinished stories and transformed it into the beginning of a novel, *Light in August*. It is the story of an orphan, Joe Christmas, whose race is uncertain, and an unwed pregnant teenager, Lena Grove. Their lives intersect in the town of Jefferson, where Lena arrives in search of her baby's father. Passion, racial prejudice, and the hypocritical religious culture of Jefferson all play a part in the development of the story. It would prove to be one of Faulkner's most challenging stories to write.

That fall, Faulkner was invited to attend a meeting of Southern writers in Charlottesville, Virginia. According to biographer David Minter, the attention he received made him uncomfortable, especially when the conversation centered on literary talk, because he lacked the formal education of his peers. This discomfort brought out the worst in him, and he began drinking heavily.[9] It was a reaction to attention and pressure that would continue throughout his life.

Hollywood Calling

In February 1932, Faulkner finished *Light in August*. That spring, he signed a contract with MGM to work in Hollywood for six weeks, writing screenplays for movies. He planned to leave Hollywood when his contract ended, but director and producer Howard Hawks wanted to make a movie of Faulkner's story "Turn About," which had been published in the *Saturday Evening Post* a few months earlier. MGM extended his contract.

On August 7, 1932, Faulkner's father died of a heart attack. Faulkner returned to Oxford to help his mother with her financial affairs, and he discovered that his father had left only enough money to support his widow for about a year. Faulkner would have to provide for his mother after that.

Old Interests, New Opportunities

Faulkner's life was busy in 1933. His work in Hollywood finally gave him enough financial success to pursue a passion left over from his World War I days. He began taking flying lessons. He bought a small airplane in May and received his pilot's wings in December. Two of his stories made it to the cinema that year. The movie *Today We Live* premiered in April. In May *The Story of Temple Drake*, based on the novel *Sanctuary*, was released.

The most significant event in his personal life, though, came in the middle of the year, when Estelle gave birth to a healthy baby girl. Faulkner had always loved children and had great affection for Estelle's daughter, Victoria, and her son, Malcolm. He had mourned the loss of his infant daughter, Alabama, but now was overjoyed with the arrival of the new baby, whom they named Jill.

The year 1934 was a productive year for Faulkner as a writer. He was working on a novel, he had a second collection of short stories published, and he began work on a new series of short stories about the Civil War. He called his novel *Absalom, Absalom!* and told his editor it was "[t]he story of a man who wanted a son through pride, and got too many of them and they destroyed him."[10] Before he finished it, however, he turned his attention to a different novel, *Pylon*, one that he could write more quickly. *Pylon* was a story about

Faulkner is pictured here in 1934, the year he worked on his novel *Absalom! Absalom!*.

MORALITY STANDARDS

Sanctuary was blasted by critics and religious groups for its violent and sexual content. Likewise, the movie adaptation, *The Story of Temple Drake*, was controversial. The film was banned in both Ohio and Pennsylvania. When the Production Code Administration began enforcing morality standards the following year (1934), the film was not allowed to be re-released and was not seen again until the 1950s.[11]

barnstorming pilots, and its climax was based on an air show crash in which a friend of Faulkner's had died.

Difficulties

The next several years were spent in much the same pattern. Faulkner worked on novels when he could, but he often found himself in need of quick cash and turned to short stories and to Hollywood contracts to stay afloat financially. Despite several periods with Twentieth Century Fox in which he earned as much as one thousand dollars a week, he still had a hard time keeping up with the expenses of Rowan Oak and with Estelle's expensive tastes. In Hollywood, Faulkner began a relationship with Howard Hawks' secretary, Meta Carpenter. Despite his affair with Meta, Faulkner would not consider divorcing Estelle for fear of losing contact with his daughter, Jill.

A personal tragedy also contributed to Faulkner's troubles. His younger brother, Dean, shared his interest in flying, and in the summer of 1935, Faulkner sold his plane to Dean. Just a few months later, Dean was killed in a crash in the plane, and Faulkner blamed himself. Dean's wife was pregnant, and

Faulkner would later assume responsibility for the child's education.

Absalom, Absalom! did not come as quickly for Faulkner as his previous novels. Faulkner worked on it through all of 1935 and finished it in January 1936. Afterward, he went on a drinking spree that ended with his admission to a hospital for rehabilitation.

His relationship with Estelle remained strained. He returned to Hollywood in February, where he continued his affair with Meta Carpenter. Estelle continued to spend money lavishly, as Faulkner worked harder and harder to pay their bills. *Absalom, Absalom!* was published in October of 1936. As it became clear to Meta that Faulkner would never divorce Estelle, she became involved with a German pianist named Wolfgang Rebner. They married in April 1937. Faulkner turned again to heavy drinking, and his work began to suffer. His contract in Hollywood was not renewed.

Faulkner began work on another novel, but then he made a trip to New York to meet with his new editor, Saxe Commins, and also to meet Meta and her new husband as they returned from their honeymoon. Seeing Meta with her new husband proved to be too much for Faulkner. He stayed in his hotel room in New York, drinking. A friend discovered him unconscious, with a bad burn on his back, apparently from falling onto a steam heating pipe in his room. The injury would require skin grafts, and the recovery would be long and painful.

"One Matchless Time"

When he was well enough to travel, Faulkner returned home to continue work on the new novel, which would later be called *The Wild Palms*. The book is the story of an unhappy couple, Charlotte Rittenmeyer and Harry Wilbourne. Years later, Faulkner would say that he wrote *The Wild Palms* "in order to try to stave off what I thought was heart-break."[12]

Another collection of Faulkner's stories, *The Unvanquished*, was published in early 1938. It consisted of a series of stories set in the Civil War that had previously been published in the *Saturday Evening Post*. He finished *The Wild Palms* and submitted it to his editor at Random House. He also wrote the short story "Barn Burning" and began work on a novel that would be the first of three in a trilogy about the Snopes family.

By this time, Faulkner had at last begun to receive recognition in the literary community. In January of 1939, he was elected to the National Institute of Arts and Letters. That same month, he was interviewed by *Time* magazine, and his photo appeared on its cover. "Barn Burning" appeared in *Harper's Bazaar* in June of that year, and it was later given the O. Henry Award as the best story of the year. Later in his life, Faulkner would fondly refer to this period, when stories came quickly and often to him, as his "one matchless time."[13]

5

Examining Three Short Stories: "A Rose for Emily," "Barn Burning," and "The Bear"

Despite his successes in the world of publishing, Faulkner still struggled to support his growing family and remodel Rowan Oak to make it livable. The Great Depression continued. Publishers paid low advances to authors, and book sales were slow. To increase his income, Faulkner began writing short stories to submit to national magazines that were still paying authors well. His stories were well received by magazines like *Forum, Scribner's,* and the *Saturday Evening Post.*

Between January 1930 and January 1932, Faulkner's notes indicate that he submitted forty-two stories for publication. Of these, twenty were accepted during this period, and ten more were published later. His income from just one story sold to the *Saturday Evening Post*, $750, was more than the total he made for his first four novels.[1] During the 1930s, Faulkner's skills as a short-story writer improved. Some of his stories were accepted by magazine editors only on the condition that he revise them. According to Faulkner scholar Hans H. Skei, revising helped Faulkner refine his skills. "Faulkner's general growth as a craftsman, in all genres, [was] due to practice and growing familiarity with his fictional kingdom and people."[2] The economy of words found in short stories for magazines required Faulkner to alter his style in some ways, especially with regard to long sentences and long passages of description. Dr. Edmond Volpe, a literary scholar, points out that many of Faulkner's novels grew from short stories, like *The Sound and the Fury*, or were compilations of short stories, like "Go Down, Moses" and "The Unvanquished." Volpe believes that "Faulkner is primarily a short story writer . . . his talent was not for the long narrative."[3]

Examining "A Rose for Emily"

The first story Faulkner was able to sell to a national magazine is widely regarded as one of his best. It has been reprinted in literature textbooks and other collections of stories more than any other of Faulkner's stories. It was also the first of Faulkner's published stories to feature the town of Jefferson. In it, Faulkner studies not only the character of one woman, but also the character of an entire Southern town as its nineteenth-century ideals come in conflict with twentieth-century life.

The story begins with the death of Miss Emily Grierson, and the statement that no one had seen the inside of her house in at least ten years, except for Miss Emily herself and her manservant. Our narrator, who speaks for the townspeople, reveals that Miss Emily has been "a tradition, a duty, and a care; a sort of hereditary obligation upon the town," since 1894 (about forty years before the time of the story) when her father died and the mayor declared that Miss Emily would never have to pay property tax on her house.[4]

The narrator views Miss Emily's story through the changing attitudes of the townspeople. Miss Emily's proud

Faulkner bought Rowan Oak in 1930. The house, originally built in 1844, required a great deal of renovation and caused the writer financial hardship.

and stern father drove away all her suitors when she was young, leaving her alone and poor when he died. Because of the Griersons' pride, the townspeople have disliked Miss Emily in the past, but now they begin to pity her. Miss Emily's only romance comes after her father's death, when she begins to keep company with a Yankee foreman of a construction company, Homer Barron. Their relationship creates a scandal in Jefferson, but the townspeople at last have hope for Miss Emily when it appears that she is getting ready to be married. She purchases a fancy toiletry set, clothing, and nightshirt—and arsenic from the druggist. One evening Homer enters Miss Emily's front door. After that, he is never seen again.

In the years since Homer's disappearance, Miss Emily has stayed in her house. The only person she sees is the manservant who brings her groceries and cooked her meals. When she finally dies at the age of seventy-four, the ladies of the town come to prepare for the funeral, and the servant walks out the back door and disappears. After the funeral, the townspeople open the locked upstairs room. There they find the remains of Homer's body in the bed, still wearing the nightshirt. The rotted remains look as though the body had "once lain in the attitude of embrace."[5] In an indention on the pillow beside the body is a long strand of Miss Emily's gray hair.

Conflict of Values

As he did in *The Sound and the Fury*, Faulkner explores the conflict between the traditions and values of the antebellum South and modern values. Mr. Grierson was a veteran of the Civil War, and his family "held themselves a little too high for what they really were."[6] In the Southern tradition, the father should have absolute control over his house, especially his daughter, who is expected to remain pure until she marries a man her father approves of. When her father dies, Emily is so used to being a daughter that she does not know how to be her own woman. At first, she even denies he is dead. After three days, she finally lets people into the house to remove the body. The townspeople recognize that Emily is made a prisoner by this tradition, and so they begin to pity her.

When she begins to enjoy her independence and be her own person, Emily finds that she cannot break out of the traditional role. When she cuts her hair and rides around with Homer Barron in the buggy, her neighbors agree that she has crossed the line of acceptable behavior. The townspeople send the Baptist minister to call on her and send for her Alabama relatives to come and set her straight. The only way Emily can regain her proper status is through marriage, but Homer has told others that he is "not a marrying man."[7] Emily is a woman who wants to be loved. When she knows that her last opportunity for affection is about to slip away, she must find some way to keep Homer with her forever. The solution seems only logical to her. All her life, Emily was taught that appearance was everything, so she must find a way to salvage her dignity, at least in her own mind. She holds her head high when she goes to the druggist for poison.

Despite the gruesome ending of the story, Emily is a sympathetic character, held to a false standard that will not allow her to fully live her life. When questioned about the title of the story, Faulkner said the rose was a gesture of sympathy. "[H]ere was a woman who had had a tragedy . . . I pitied her and this was a salute."[8]

Narrative Voice

Emily's tragedy is only half of this story. The other half comes through the narrator who represents the townspeople of Jefferson. According to literary scholar Edmond Volpe, "Faulkner, ingeniously, makes the community a living entity, a character with a past, a personality, a memory, and feelings," through his use of the narrator.[9] The townspeople represent the Southern tradition and its hypocrisy. While they recognize the tragedy of Emily's situation, they still expect her to conform to tradition, and they have only contempt for her when she tries to break free of it.

The people of Jefferson are unable to break free of the past, just as Emily is. When the town fathers try to collect the taxes on the property, she tells them to go talk to Colonel Sartoris, even though he has been dead for ten years. Their sense of duty to the past prevents them from forcing her to pay the taxes. When neighbors complain about the smell coming from her house, they try to explain it as a dead rat killed by the manservant, but they all know the truth. As the narrator tells it, the whole town knows about the arsenic Emily purchased, and they know the neighbor who saw Homer go into Emily's house that night and never come out.

It is likely that Faulkner identified with the narrator who represents the people of Jefferson. Although he seemed to resist the traditions of the South as he tried to escape from Oxford to spend time in New Orleans and New York City, he always came back. As he portrayed the darkest side of Southern traditions, Faulkner still clung to the traditions of his family, struggling to recreate the "big house" of his great-grandfather as he renovated Rowan Oak. Volpe says that "A Rose for Emily" is "a masterful, moving expression of Faulkner's own ambivalent feelings for the South, and a haunting revelation of the South's struggle with a legacy that dehumanizes and cripples its proud, tragic heirs."[10]

A painting of Faulkner in his riding habit hangs in the parlor of Rowan Oak. In many ways, he clung to Southern traditions despite his conflicted feelings about the South.

The Snopes Family in "Barn Burning"

By 1938 Faulkner had a new work in mind, one that would take him three books and many years to complete: the story of the Snopes family. That autumn, Faulkner described the beginning of *The Hamlet* for his editor, Robert Haas. In the story, the youngest Snopes boy "tries to keep his father from setting fire to his landlord's barn, believes he has caused his father to be shot, and runs away from home."[11] *The Hamlet* does not begin with the story "Barn Burning" as its first chapter. Instead, Faulkner sent the story to his agent, Harold Ober, to sell it to a magazine. Ober sold the story to *Harper's Magazine* on the sixth try. Some of the editors who rejected it described it as "too depressing."[12] Critics today consider it one of Faulkner's best stories.

The story is told by an omniscient narrator who sees the story mostly through the eyes of ten-year-old Sarty Snopes, whose full name is Colonel Sartoris Snopes. The narrator goes beyond Sarty's viewpoint, however, by telling us about the past and also about the future. The story begins in a country store, where Sarty's father, Abner ("Ab") Snopes, has been brought before the justice of the peace, accused of setting fire to a neighbor's barn. The neighbor's testimony suggests that Ab is guilty, and Sarty's fear of being called to tell what he knows seems to confirm that. There is no real evidence, and Ab is instructed to leave the area and not come back.

Expecting this outcome, the Snopes family and their possessions are already loaded and waiting on a wagon outside. Sarty; his older brother, Flem; his mother; aunt; and two sisters are ready to move on because of Ab's actions. This is at least the twelfth move that Sarty can remember in his short life. When the family is stopped for the night, Ab takes Sarty away from the rest of the family. He accuses the boy of intending to betray him that day and hits him hard, but without anger. This cold cruelty is the basis of Ab's personality.

Their next stop is a sharecropper cabin on the property of Major de Spain. Soon after their arrival, Ab decides to go to the big house to meet his employer. Ab deliberately steps in horse manure and tracks it onto the expensive white carpet. Later, when Ab learns that he will have to give de Spain some of his crop to pay for the rug, Sarty worries that his father will take revenge. After dark, Ab and Flem gather oil, kerosene, and burning candles to burn de Spain's barn. Sarty runs up the road to warn the de Spain household. De Spain rushes from the house, gets on his horse, and rides past Sarty toward the barn. Sarty hears two shots, and he assumes his father is dead. Although he grieves for his father, he also is relieved to be finally free of him. The story ends as he walks away without looking back.

"The Old Fierce Pull of Blood"

The primary conflicts in "Barn Burning" concern individual power. Ab Snopes has always been at the bottom of the social structure for a white man in the South. Others have the power of money or the power of law on their side. Ab has only his anger. In his family, he exerts control through physical violence and through the power of "blood" loyalty. Outside his family, his only power comes through violence, and he creates conflicts solely for the purpose of taking revenge. His violence is not fueled by anger. When he strikes Sarty, he does it "with the flat of his hand on the side of the head, hard but without heat."[13] When his wife tries to stop him from going to de Spain's barn, he "flung her back, not savagely or viciously, just hard, into the wall."[14]

Sarty has always been held to his father's will by "the old fierce pull of blood."[15] He identifies with his father, and his father's enemy is his own. When Sarty first sees the de Spain house, however, he senses a greater power than his father's. He hopes that finally there is someone whom his father cannot touch. He thinks maybe things will be different for his father now: *"Maybe it will even change him now from what maybe he couldn't help but be."*[16] Sarty's brother has already given in to his father's will and joins him in burning barns. Ab senses that Sarty is trying to decide if he will accept Ab's will or rebel. Ab tries to intimidate Sarty with violence and with appeals to his family loyalty. Finally, Sarty discovers his own power, and he is at last free, even though it will not be easy for him to be on his own. In this interpretation, Sarty's choice is not really a matter of right or wrong; it is his acceptance of his own individuality and personal power.

motif

An object or element that appears frequently throughout a work of literature and may suggest a specific idea to the reader.

Symbolism in "Barn Burning"

As in other stories, Faulkner uses some motifs, or repeated images, in the story to suggest a deeper meaning. In the opening scene, Sarty crouches in the general store, aware of cans of meat with pictures of red devils on the labels. This initial image is not important to the events in the story, but it does create a suggestion of evil that Faulkner uses throughout the story. In this interpretation, good and evil play a role in Sarty's choice at the end of the story.

Volpe points to several of Faulkner's descriptions of Ab Snopes that suggest satanic images. For example, Ab is always dressed in black and appears stiff. In folklore, the devil does not cast a shadow. Sarty sees his father as though he were a flat silhouette cut from tin, "as though, sideways to the sun, it would cast no shadow."[17]

When Ab reaches up to knock on the door of the de Spain house, his hand is "like a curled claw."[18] Ab's coat is made of "broadcloth which had once been black but which now had the friction-glazed greenish cast of the bodies of old house flies."[19] Because the devil is sometimes called "The Lord of the Flies," this description of Ab further supports the suggestion of Faulkner's deliberate use of the satanic images.[20]

As Volpe also points out, Ab seeks to make everyone do his will. He has already succeeded with the rest of the family. Sarty's free will is a threat to his father's power. According to the Bible, Satan was an angel cast out of heaven because of his pride. Ab's violence is also a product of his pride and his tool of destruction is fire.[21] Seen in this way, Sarty's decision to defy his father and break away from him could symbolize salvation. At the end of the story, the dawn comes and Sarty wakes to begin his journey to a new life.

"The Bear": Story or Chapter?

Faulkner's book *Go Down, Moses* was originally published as *Go Down, Moses and Other Stories*, thus suggesting that the volume was a collection of seven stories rather than a novel. Many critics have considered the book this way, although later editions of the book dropped the last three words of the title at Faulkner's request because he considered the book one story instead of seven.[22] Nevertheless, the section entitled "The Bear" is often considered as a story independent from the rest of the book. An earlier form of the story, entitled "Lion: A Story," appeared in *Harper's Magazine* in December 1935. Another version appeared in *The Saturday Evening Post* with the title "The Bear" in May 1942, about the same time the book was published.

The events and setting of the story—a bear hunt in the unsettled timberland of Mississippi—reflect Faulkner's interest in both. According to his brother John, Faulkner went on a similar hunt during the early 1930s. "He was invited to go on General Stone's deer-and-bear hunt, at his lodge below Batesville in the virgin bottom lands of the Mississippi Delta," said John. When asked what kind of rifle he would take to shoot a bear, he said he did not plan to take a rifle. "He said if he met a bear in the woods he didn't want to have to take the time to throw away a gun before he could start running."[23] According to his brother, Faulkner participated almost every year after that first invitation and became a competent woodsman. It is not surprising that the story "Lion" and later "The Bear" would come out of these experiences.

Unusual Narrative Structure

In *Go Down, Moses*, "The Bear" is divided into five chapters. The first three are about Ike's apprenticeship in the woods and the hunt for Old Ben; the fourth is an extended conversation between Ike and his cousin Cass, concerning the truth of their family history; the fifth describes Ike's last trip to the woods. The fourth section interrupts the time sequence of the story. The first three sections begin when Ike is sixteen, and section five takes place when Ike is eighteen, but Ike is twenty-one at the beginning of the fourth section.

In the context of *Go Down, Moses*, the fourth section ties "The Bear" to the rest of the novel as it explains the history of the McCaslin family and the blood relationship between the white McCaslin family and the Beauchamp family, who were their slaves. It also reveals Ike's revulsion for the acts of

Faulkner uses symbolism and satanic imagery to convey the evil nature of Ab Snopes in "Barn Burning."

his grandfather, who fathered a daughter, Tomasina, with his slave, then fathered a son with Tomasina.

Years after its publication, Faulkner commented on the reading of "The Bear" as a story separate from *Go Down, Moses*. He said that the fourth section is "part of the novel but not part of the story . . . It doesn't belong with the short story."[24] Taken out of the context of the book, section four is difficult to read and understand, especially given the complexity of Faulkner's narrative. Within it is one sentence of sixteen hundred words, one of the longest sentences in the English language. This section of "The Bear" explores the theme of race relations that is central to *Go Down, Moses*, but it is not essential to the main plot of the bear hunt, or to most of the other themes of "The Bear," which can be examined without it.

Ike's Story

"The Bear" is the story of young Isaac ("Ike") McCaslin. The main part of the story begins in 1883 when Ike is sixteen years old, but it also flashes back to 1877, when Ike was ten and was allowed to go on his first hunt. Ike is mentored by Sam Fathers, an elderly man who is part American Indian, part white, and part African American. Although the hunters are principally hunting deer, they are also pursuing Old Ben, a gigantic black bear with a foot disfigured by a bear trap. The bear has become almost legendary because it is smart and strong. Sam believes they will someday hunt the bear, but not until they have the right dog to corner it and bring it to bay.

Sam teaches Ike the skills he needs to survive in the wilderness. When Ike is thirteen years old, he shoots his first deer, and Sam marks the boy's face with the blood of the deer as a rite of passage. Sam captures a wild dog that he believes will help them hunt Old Ben. He names the dog Lion, and he allows Ike's cousin Boon Hogganbeck to take over the care of the dog.

When Ike is sixteen, Lion is finally ready for the hunt. He catches the bear's scent and chases him through the woods as the hunting party follows. When Lion at last corners Old Ben and lunges at his throat, Old Ben rips open the belly of the dog with its claws. Ike raises his gun, but he cannot get a clear shot of the bear. Boon rushes in to save Lion. He jumps on the bear's back and stabs it in the heart with his knife. As the bear falls dead, Sam Fathers also collapses. Lion dies, and they bury him in the woods. When Sam dies a few days later, Ike and Boon take his body to the same spot and bury it next to Lion. They also bury a tin box containing Old Ben's mangled paw.

Two years later, Ike returns to the woods. Major de Spain has sold the land to a lumber company, and Ike goes to visit

FAULKNER THE HUNTER

Faulkner was an avid hunter from his childhood on. When he first received notification that he had won the Nobel Prize, he sent a message to Sweden declining the invitation to appear to accept the award, then left for a hunting trip. Fortunately he was convinced by friends, and by the US State Department, to attend the ceremony. According to one story, "After the hunters returned from deer camp, one of Faulkner's companions wrote the King of Sweden (who had given Faulkner his award in Stockholm) and invited him to next year's deer camp to hunt and share 'a coon and collard dinner, for if you are a friend of William Faulkner's, you are a friend of ours.' The king politely declined the invitation."[25]

Sam's grave one last time. At the grave site, he leaves some tobacco and peppermint candy, which Sam loved, then walks away. At the end of the story, Ike finds Boon Hogganbeck hammering at the dismembered pieces of his gun, while dozens of squirrels scramble in the tree above him. Boon shouts, "Dont touch a one of them! They're mine!"[26]

Themes in "The Bear"

As in many of his novels and stories, Faulkner uses the theme of a boy's initiation into manhood in "The Bear." Ten-year-old Ike is brought to the woods "to earn for himself from the wilderness the name and state of hunter."[27] Although his older cousin Cass Edmonds has become his father figure in place of his deceased father, his spiritual mentor is Sam Fathers. When Ike first kills a deer, Sam Fathers marks Ike with the blood of the deer as a sign that he is now a hunter.

When the time comes to hunt Old Ben with the help of Lion, Ike has earned the respect of the other hunters. General Compson decides that Ike will ride Katie, the only mule that is not afraid of the scent of the bear. When Cass objects, the general says, "I want Ike to ride Katie. He's already a better woodsman than you or me either. . . ."[28] When the rest of the men break camp, Ike wants to stay behind with Sam Fathers. Again, General Compson recognizes that Ike has earned the right because of his connection to Sam and to the wilderness.

In the last section, Ike uses only instinct to find the place where Sam and Lion are buried. He does not stop to mourn there, but only pauses briefly, knowing that the place is "no abode of the dead because there was no death, not Lion and not Sam: not held fast in earth but free in earth and not in earth but of earth . . . [29] As a man and a hunter, Ike now identifies fully with Sam Fathers, and he recognizes the spirit of all

Hunting was a popular pastime in the South, and one that Faulkner enjoyed. His short story "The Bear" centers around a bear hunt and a boy's coming of age.

6 The Struggling Writer

From 1939 to 1954 Faulkner experienced great advances in his career as well as great personal struggles. It seemed that no matter how successful he was in his writing, he was always just a step away from despair and depression. Unfortunately, his response to those struggles was often self-destructive behavior that affected his writing, his relationships, and his health.

In 1938 Faulkner had begun a story about the Snopes family of Yoknapatawpha. According to biographer David Minter, writing the first book of the trilogy, *The Hamlet*, was "a striking adventure," that brought him great satisfaction.[1] He finished it in October of 1939. When it was published in April of 1940, *The Hamlet* did not receive very good reviews. It would be many years before the other two volumes of the trilogy, *The Town* and *The Mansion*, would be finished.

Financial troubles continued to worry Faulkner. His obligation for back taxes was great enough that he feared he would lose Rowan Oak.[2] His worry led to drinking binges, which in turn interfered with his writing. His short stories were not selling well. He now had financial obligations for his mother and his brother's widow and daughter, as well as his own family. As World War II was building in Europe, Faulkner was feeling his age and regretting that he never saw action in World War I. He even accepted a brief job of teaching navigation and radio operation to military volunteers in Mississippi.

Faulkner in 1939. Despite his professional success, the writer's personal woes led to alcohol abuse and infidelity.

The Sins of the Father in *Go Down, Moses*

Faulkner's next writing project was a group of stories about the McCaslin family. Like *The Unvanquished*, the stories tied together. Faulkner spent 1940 and 1941 working on the collection, which became *Go Down, Moses and Other Stories*. The book tells the story of the McCaslins, the bloodline from Lucius Quintus Carothers McCaslin, who has three children with his wife, one child with his slave, and even a child by his own illegitimate daughter. The stories examines how the guilt of Lucius's behavior is carried by the future generations of the McCaslin family.

By 1942, sales of Faulkner's novels had declined. Once again he returned to Hollywood for the income he needed. In the summer of 1942, he signed a seven-year contract with Warner Brothers. The studio agreed to pay him a salary of only three hundred dollars per week, far less than he had made at other times. It would be his longest contract with any Hollywood studio and one he would regret. In the fall of 1943, he requested a leave of several months.

When he returned to Oxford, he began work on a story he called "Who?" It would be very different from the Yoknapatawpha books. He described it as a fable in which Christ is reincarnated as a soldier during World War I. He finished an early draft of the story in 1944 but immediately began rewriting it, knowing he was not nearly finished with it. He set the story aside to return to script writing in Hollywood.

Renewed Interest in Faulkner's Work

During 1944, critic Malcolm Cowley wrote a feature on Faulkner for the *New York Times Book Review*. By this time, many of Faulkner's novels were out of print, but the essay by Cowley brought new interest in his books. Soon after, Cowley first new book since *Go Down, Moses*, six years earlier. It had great commercial success, selling more than fifteen thousand copies in the first year.[5] In July, MGM purchased the film rights to the book for fifty thousand dollars.[6] The following year, MGM sent a movie crew to Oxford to make the film there. Financially, it was a turning point in Faulkner's life.

In November 1949, *Knight's Gambit*, a collection of Faulkner's detective stories, was published, along with new editions of *The Wild Palms*, *The Hamlet*, and *Go Down, Moses*. Also in 1949, Faulkner met a college student named Joan Williams who wanted to become a writer. Her aunt and uncle were friends of Faulkner's, and she visited Rowan Oak to meet

Faulkner receives the 1949 Nobel Prize in Literature from King Gustaf VI of Sweden.

Faulkner. They began to exchange letters. After Christmas, she agreed to meet him on his boat, and a few weeks later they met in New York. Soon gossip about their relationship came to Estelle. Despite his wife's anger, Faulkner continued to write letters to Williams and went to meet her whenever he could.

Recognition

In 1950, Faulkner at last began receiving recognition for his contribution to literature. That year he received the Howells Medal for Distinguished Work in American Fiction. He also was awarded the Nobel Prize in Literature, presented to him in Sweden that December. Although Faulkner did not want to make the trip, he was pressured by the Swedish ambassador to the United States, by his wife, and even by the US State Department. Finally, his daughter, Jill, convinced her father that he should go and take her. She was about to graduate from high school and had never been out of the country. He agreed to go.

Before leaving, though, Faulkner went on a drinking binge and then came down with a bad cold. It was a hard trip for him, and, as usual, having so much attention focused on him was difficult. At the award ceremony, he spoke so quickly and quietly that no one in the room understood what he had said. His speech was published in the newspaper the following day and now, according to biographer Jay Parini, "has become the most famous speech by any American writer to receive the Nobel."[7]

Faulkner dedicated his speech to young men and women in the audience who wanted to write and who might someday be standing where he was, accepting a Nobel Prize in the future. He reminded them that, in spite of world problems such as the Cold War, the only things really worth writing about were "the problems of the human heart in conflict with itself." Without that in mind, the writer "writes not of love but of lust, of defeats in which nobody loses anything of value, of victories without hope and, worst of all, without pity or compassion." In his optimistic conclusion, Faulkner announced that he could not believe that man would be destroyed. "I believe that man will not merely endure: he will prevail. He is immortal, not because he alone among creatures has an inexhaustible voice, but because he has a soul, a spirit capable of compassion and sacrifice and endurance."[8]

New Work, More Honors

In the summer of 1950, another volume of short stories, entitled *Collected Stories of William Faulkner,* was published. It would earn Faulkner the National Book Award. In the meantime, Faulkner had been working on a story he had first begun in 1933, which he called "Requiem for a Nun." He now took the idea and developed it as a play. Later, he realized it should be a novel, and he kept working on it, eventually creating a play within a novel. The book continued the story of Temple Drake from *Sanctuary*. At the beginning of 1951, Faulkner decided to set aside his work on *A Fable*, so that he could concentrate more on *Requiem for a Nun*. For the months of February and March, though, he had to return to Hollywood for more script work. At this time, he was working on the movie *The Left Hand of God* and earning two thousand dollars a week.[9] In April, he made a trip to France to do some research for the final scene of *A Fable*. In France, he spent time with Else Jonsson, an attractive woman he had met in Sweden when he accepted the Nobel Prize.

Shortly after the trip, he learned he had been awarded the French Legion of Honor by French president Vincent Auriol.

Faulkner finished the manuscript of *Requiem for a Nun* in June, then spent much of June and July in New York working on a stage adaptation of the story. In September, *Requiem for a Nun* was published in book form, although the production of the play was delayed because of lack of funding.

In the spring of 1952, Faulkner was invited to a cultural festival in Paris. He had hoped that his play *Requiem for a Nun* would be performed there, but the organizing committee was unable to raise the money needed for the production. Still, Faulkner felt obligated to attend the festival, having received the Legion of Honor award.

Pain, Alcohol, and Depression

After the festival, Faulkner was suffering a great deal from back pain from his old injury. His usual treatment for pain was whiskey, and the combination of pain and alcohol led to a hospital stay in France. It was the beginning of a period of decline in his physical health. When Faulkner finally returned home that June, he was ready to return to work on *A Fable*, but by September, the pain returned, and he was hospitalized in Memphis. In October, he suffered a fall down the stairs at Rowan Oak. After another hospital stay, he was fitted with a steel brace for his back. Near the end of November, he traveled to Princeton to stay with his editor Saxe Commins in order to continue work on *A Fable*. Again the pain flared up, and Faulkner was again admitted to the hospital. This time he received electroshock therapy.

In 1953, Faulkner was still working on *A Fable*, but he was hospitalized again for pain and alcohol in both January and March. That April, Faulkner returned home when Estelle suffered a hemorrhage and heart attack. Although her condition was serious, she recovered in a few weeks, and Faulkner returned to New York, where he worked daily on the novel at the office of Saxe Commins.

Faulkner worked all summer to finish the novel, and he wrote a detailed outline of the plot on the wall of his study at Rowan Oak. Estelle took Jill on a trip to Mexico in order to give Faulkner the solitude he seemed to need. Left alone, however, he soon lapsed into depression again, according to biographer Joseph Blotner, which he treated with a combination of alcohol and a powerful sedative, Seconal.[10] In September, he was hospitalized in Memphis to undergo treatment for his chemical dependencies. He stayed only a week before returning to Rowan Oak, then relapsed and required another hospital stay just a few weeks later.

By this time, Faulkner had begun to feel the effects of his fame in a loss of his privacy. In the fall of 1953, *Life* published a two-part feature on Faulkner. When the reporter, Robert Coughlan, had contacted him, Faulkner had refused to be interviewed, and he did his best to stop the article's publication. The *Life* article also had photos of Faulkner's family and his house. He was angry that people in Oxford had cooperated with the magazine's staff and had shared their stories of his family and childhood.

His Next "Tour de Force"

In November 1953, Faulkner returned to Princeton to work one last time on *A Fable*. He stayed at the home of Saxe Commins and his wife, where they allowed him to spread out the manuscript and make revisions. Just days after his arrival, he dated the final page of the book that had taken him so many years to write. In 1954 he worked on corrections to the manuscript, and the book was published in August of that year. Although *A Fable* had taken many years of work, Faulkner had

Faulkner poses at the airport with his daughter Jill, age seventeen. Jill convinced her father to make the trip to Sweden to receive the Nobel Prize in 1950.

Science Monitor said that it "does not rank with Faulkner's best work."[2] Charles J. Rolo, writing in *The Atlantic Monthly* said: "The plot and subplots are poorly integrated, and the people are for the most part only vaguely suggested." He called the story "spurious and unreal—a heroically ambitious failure."[3]

Some critics, however, saw more in *A Fable*. Herbert Cahoon of *Library Journal* had high praise for the book, calling it "powerful and intricate." He rated the book "Highly recommended."[4] Ultimately, Faulkner's book would gain acceptance,

In 1955 Faulkner received the National Book Award for Fiction for *A Fable*. Standing with him are Joseph Wood Krutch (left), who received the award for nonfiction, and Wallace Stevens (right), who won for his poetry.

earning its author both the National Book Award for Fiction and the Pulitzer Prize for Fiction in 1955.

War and Peace in *A Fable*

On a morning in May 1918, a French general commands his regiment to attack the enemy, but the soldiers lay down their weapons and emerge from their trenches unarmed. Their enemies, the German soldiers, do the same thing, and the battlefield falls silent. Angered and humiliated, the French general requests that all three thousand soldiers be executed on a charge of mutiny. He learns that the mutiny was planned by a single corporal and his twelve followers.

Alarmed that their war can be disrupted so easily, the commanding officers of France, Britain, America, and even Germany meet to discuss how they will handle the situation. They all agree that they cannot allow the war to end on these terms.

The corporal, his twelve followers, and the rest of the regiment are jailed in Paris to await their executions. Their relatives from the surrounding countryside gather in the city. They form a mob, angry not at the military leaders who threaten to execute the soldiers, but at the corporal and his followers who have caused these events. In the crowd are three woman related to the corporal: his two sisters and his wife (although she is also called his fiancée).

From the women, the supreme commander of the French army learns that the corporal is his illegitimate son. He calls in the corporal and offers to save him, revealing that the corporal and his men had been betrayed by one of the twelve. He offers to execute the betrayer in the corporal's place along with the remaining eleven, and then free the rest of the three thousand. The corporal refuses.

The corporal is executed by a firing squad, and his body is taken by his sisters to be buried on their farm. That night, the farm is hit in an artillery attack. The next day, the sisters find fragments of the coffin, but no trace of the body.

After the war, France prepares a monument for the Tomb of the Unknown Soldier in Paris. A group of soldiers is sent to retrieve a body for the tomb. They are led to the farm next to that of the corporal's sisters, where they find a body, presumably the body of the corporal.

The book ends with the burial of the supreme general. An English runner, who understood the mission of the corporal and knows the way the generals prolonged the war, disrupts the ceremony. He is beaten by the crowd, but insists, "I'm not going to die. Never."[5]

A "Difficult" and "Obscure" Narrative

Many readers find *A Fable* a difficult book to read. As he often does, Faulkner uses an omniscient narrator, one who is able to report the thoughts and feelings of many characters and can move from place to place, as well as backward and forward in time. Although this allows the author the greatest freedom in telling the story, it can make the sequence of events confusing for the reader.

The main plot of the story covers seven days. Faulkner identifies the days of the week in the story in his chapter headings, but he begins with Wednesday, then goes back to Monday night, then moves to Tuesday night. The story then takes the reader back to events on Monday, then Tuesday, and so forth. The second half of the book follows more sequentially, but it sometimes skips from one scene to another abruptly, without identifying characters immediately.

Some readers may find a reader's guide with a chronological summary of the story's events helpful in understanding the plot. Edmond Volpe's *Reader's Guide to William Faulkner: The Novels* includes an appendix with the scenes of the book arranged in their order of occurrence and page numbers corresponding to the 1954 edition.

Faulkner's personal knowledge of World War I allows him to create realistic and detailed descriptions of settings and weaponry. His omniscient narrator, in the minds of his soldier characters, follows their thoughts, including their use of military jargon in their descriptions and their dialogue. Although much of this specialized language is explained or else becomes clear as the narrative progresses, it can be confusing.

jargon

Specialized language or terms related to a particular activity, career area, or field that people outside that field might not be familiar with.

As always, Faulkner is a master at creating visual images for the reader through his descriptions. In places, he inserts long passages of description into scenes of action, so that one character might speak to another, but the reply comes only after a long paragraph or a full page of description.

These difficulties in Faulkner's narrative style caused critics to doubt that readers would really appreciate the story. A reviewer in the publication *Kirkus* commented: "Creatively, it is an extraordinary achievement with its underlying commentary of an unready world. Practically, it is difficult reading, and often obscure."[6] Riley Hughes, in *Catholic World* predicted that *A Fable* would be "the most unread best-seller of 1954."[7]

Faulkner wrote notes for *A Fable* that he posted on the wall at Rowan Oak. Today those notes can still be seen by visitors to the home.

Biblical Allegory in *A Fable*

Faulkner fashioned the plot of his novel on the story of the last week of the life of Christ to create an allegory. In speaking of the novel to students in Japan, Faulkner said, "I used that form, I used a story which had been proven to be one that did move man, which was that part at which the father must choose between the son's sacrifice or saving the son, as one of the most moving tragedies that can happen to the human breast."[8]

There are many elements of the story and details of the corporal (the Christ figure of the novel) that make the similarities to the biblical story of Christ unmistakable. Here are just a few of them:

- The corporal has a group of twelve followers, as Christ did.
- The corporal was born in a stable on Christmas.
- The corporal and his twelve followers share dinner before the execution.
- One of the twelve is revealed as a betrayer.
- On the third day after the corporal's death his body is missing.
- He is attended by three women.

Despite the many similarities, there are some significant differences between the story of Christ and the story of the corporal.

- The corporal is not the son of God but the illegitimate son of a flawed man.
- The corporal does not perform any miracles.
- The body of the corporal does not really disappear; it is blown by artillery onto the neighboring farm.

These differences are important, since Christ's miracles and resurrection are the most basic beliefs of Christianity and make him more than mortal man. These discrepancies suggest that Faulkner did not intend for the book to convey a strictly biblical message. Instead, he used the biblical story to illustrate the power of a man who acts according to his conscience. In an interview in 1955, Faulkner said, "No one is without Christianity, if we agree on what we mean by the word. It is every individual's individual code of behavior by means of which he makes himself a better human being than his nature wants to be, if he followed his nature only."[9]

Morality in *A Fable*

Several important ideas come out of this novel. One of the strongest is the power of the individual to follow his conscience, and his responsibility to do so. When the soldiers refuses to fight, there is no war. The English runner vows to carry this message forward, no matter the personal cost. By contrast, the supreme general has the potential for good but does not accept that responsibility, and he is corrupted by power. At the end, the quartermaster general, who saw that potential, weeps.

Faulkner described the differences between individual attitudes as "the trinity of conscience: knowing nothing, knowing but not caring, knowing and caring." He added:

The same trinity is represented in *A Fable* by the young Jewish pilot officer who said, "This is terrible. I refuse to accept it, even if I must refuse life to do so," the old French Quartermaster General who said, "This is terrible, but we can weep and bear it," and the English battalion runner who said, "This is terrible, I'm going to do something about it."[10]

The story also suggests that there is a higher morality than that which is laid down by man through his political and military leaders. The soldiers disobey the orders of their commander, knowing that mutiny is punishable by death. The corporal willingly accepts his own death as the ultimate cost in the moral choice for peace and to redeem the others who have followed him.

allegory

A story that symbolically suggests a deeper meaning because its plot, characters, and/or setting together stand for other ideas, people, or things.

Through this allegory, *A Fable* examines the roles of nations, of military leaders, and of individual soldiers in wars. The power of the common soldier is shown in the sudden silence on the battlefield, but the commanding officers cannot allow the war to end that easily. They have all built careers with honors on the battlefield. "'It wasn't we who invented war,' the group commander said. 'It was war which created us. From the loins of man's furious ineradicable greed sprang the captains and the colonels to his necessity.'"[11] They already know when the war will end. Their own greed and lust for power and rank drive them to continue war at the cost of innocent lives. This is the truth that the English runner dedicates himself to spreading.

The Inner Conflict of Man

A Fable has enough complexity to suggest different ways of looking at it. Edmonde Volpe views the book as a statement about the dual nature of man—his ability to embody opposite characteristics at the same time. Some reviewers criticized Faulkner's lack of developed characters. Riley Hughes, in *Catholic World*, called the dialogue "pretentious" and said, "the characters are mere types."[12] Volpe contends that Faulkner did this intentionally because the characters are not real people but rather symbolic of elements of human qualities.[13] Sutterfield tells the English runner, "Evil is a part of man, evil and sin and cowardice, the same as repentance and being brave. You got to believe in all of them, or believe in none of them."[14]

"Powerful" but "Murky"

Despite the awards given to *A Fable*, most critics today do not consider it one of Faulkner's best, and it has never received the amount of critical attention that has been given to *The Sound and the Fury*. Faulkner had a great deal of difficulty with the book, spending nearly a decade on it. But he felt he had something important to say. He said, "[It] was principally to try to tell what I had found in my lifetime of truth in some important way before I had to put the pen down and die."[15]

Even Malcolm Cowley, a great admirer of Faulkner's work, had reservations about *A Fable*, as expressed in his review in the *New York Herald-Tribune*. Although Cowley admitted that the book "contains some of the most powerful scenes [Faulkner] has ever conceived," he called Faulkner's theology and his style "murky" and added "there is something confused in the lesson of the book . . . Its many readers will wonder and argue about it for a long time to come."[16]

8 Faulkner's Last Years

By 1954 Faulkner's many bouts of depression, binge drinking, and physical injuries had taken a toll on his body. His years of extramarital affairs had taken a toll on his relationship with Estelle. But despite these limitations, Faulkner continued to enjoy riding and training horses. He also enjoyed his position among the leading writers of his day, and he still had more stories to write.

After finishing the manuscript of *A Fable* in November 1953, Faulkner went to see Joan Williams, who was now working as an editor at *Look* magazine. She made it clear to Faulkner that she did not want to continue their relationship. According to biographer Jay Parini, it was a hard blow to his ego, which he treated "by visiting bars and restaurants with friends."[1]

Literary Ambassador

On November 30, Faulkner left the United States on his way to Cairo, Egypt, to work on the movie *Land of the Pharaohs* with his longtime friend, director Howard Hawks. On the way, he made several stops in Europe, where he met a nineteen-year-old college student named Jean Stein, and he also spent time with Else Jonsson. On the trip, he heard from Joan Williams, who announced that she was engaged to be married. He began

Faulkner's love of horses lasted his whole life. Even as his health was deteriorating, he continued to ride whenever he could.

drinking heavily and was again hospitalized. He returned to the United States in April, ready to get back to Rowan Oak and his life in the country. He also learned that his daughter, Jill, was planning to be married to Paul Summers, a West Point graduate. He returned home to find a flurry of activity related to Jill's upcoming wedding.

A representative of the US State Department invited Faulkner to attend an international writer's conference in Brazil later that month. The trip included cocktail parties and press conferences in both Lima, Peru, and São Paulo, Brazil. Despite a drinking binge that required a two-day drying-out period in the care of a Brazilian doctor in his hotel room, Faulkner made a good impression in both countries.[2] Soon after his return, Jill was married to Paul Summers.

After the wedding, Faulkner was ready to return to his writing. He worked on some short stories and other projects for magazines. That autumn, *Life* writer Robert Coughlan, who had written the feature story that angered Faulkner a year earlier, published a book entitled *The Private World of William Faulkner*. In response, Faulkner wrote an essay he called "The American Dream: What Happened to It?" in which he blasted the press for its ability to intrude in the private lives of citizens. Although the essay was not published at the time, Faulkner would continue to use it as a speaking topic and would later revise it for publication. As 1954 drew to a close, Faulkner was spending more and more time away from home, most of it in New York with Jean Stein.

Faulkner on Social Issues

In 1955 Faulkner began to make more public appearances to discuss his work and also to make public comments on political subjects such as school integration. He wrote several letters

GUIDELINES

When Faulkner became a cultural ambassador for the United States, his drinking quickly became a problem. After he became so intoxicated at a reception in Japan he couldn't communicate, the State Department was ready to send him home. In response, an officer at the American embassy in Tokyo created a set of guidelines for managing Faulkner on these international trips. The suggestions included: "Keep several pretty young girls in the front two rows of any public appearance to keep his attention up," "Put someone in charge of his liquor at all times so that he doesn't drink too quickly," and "Do not allow him to venture out on his own without an escort." The officer was commended by J. Edgar Hoover for his work.[3]

to a Memphis newspaper criticizing Mississippi schools. The federal government had mandated integration of schools, but there was much resistance among white Southerners. Faulkner knew that the segregated schools of Mississippi were inadequate, but he believed that it would take much more than just integration to make them better. He accused the schools of being "community or state-supported babysitters," and suggested that students of all races needed to be challenged to succeed in an academic system.[4] He drew criticism from many Southerners and even received anonymous phone calls and threats. He tried to explain the racial conflict in the United States to his Swedish friend Else Jonssen: "We have much tragic trouble in Mississippi about Negroes . . . I am doing what I can. I can see the possible time when I shall have to leave my native state, something as the Jew had to flee from

Germany during Hitler."[5] Faulkner also continued to speak out against the abuses of the press on individual privacy. In April, he delivered speeches at both the University of Oregon and also the University of Montana with the title "Freedom American Style," an adaptation of the essay he had written the previous fall.

The US State Department continued to call upon Faulkner to be a kind of cultural ambassador. In August, he traveled to Japan to meet with students at the university and answer their questions about his work. After leaving Japan, he made a stop in Rome for ten days of relaxation and time with Jean Stein. He traveled throughout Germany, Italy, France, and Iceland that summer and fall. In Europe, he went to parties with Jean Stein, with other old friends, and also with authors such as Tennessee Williams.

Near the end of 1955, Faulkner was at last ready to return to writing novels. He began the second book of the Snopes trilogy he had begun in 1939 with *The Hamlet*. The new volume would be called *The Town*.

Professor and Grandfather

In the spring of 1956, Jill Faulkner Summers gave birth to a baby boy. Jill and her husband lived in Charlottesville, Virginia. Faulkner agreed to accept a position as writer-in-residence at the University of Virginia soon after his grandson's birth. The job would require him to stay in Charlottesville for several weeks each year, teaching and lecturing at the school. His appointment would begin the following January.

In the meantime, Faulkner continued to write political essays, including one called "On Fear: The South in Labor," which appeared in *Harper's* in June 1956. He also worked on *The Town*, and he sent chapters to Jean Stein for her

The 1950s were a time of great racial tension in the South, and Faulkner spoke out about issues like school desegregation. In this photo, black students walk through a crowd into a recently integrated school.

comments. He continued to comment on racial issues, but he was often criticized for his remarks. Although he spoke out against forced segregation, he also spoke against forced integration. An essay he wrote for *Ebony* magazine entitled "If I Were a Negro," took a stance that would be considered very liberal for a Southern white man, but it was far too conservative for many black leaders of the time. Faulkner called for peaceful demonstrations carried out "decently, quietly, courteously, with dignity and without violence."[6] The essay drew anger from black activists.

Near the end of the summer, Faulkner finished *The Town*. His agent sold the last chapter of the book as a story to *The Saturday Evening Post*, for three thousand dollars. The magazine would publish it with the title "The Waifs" in the May 4, 1957, issue.

In February of 1957, Faulkner moved to Charlottesville to begin his new job at the University of Virginia. He seemed to enjoy this new role and often took walks around the campus. He worked mostly with graduate students in the English department, but he also held question-and-answer sessions with other students. He and Estelle moved into a house near the college. Faulkner made frequent visits to a nearby stable to ride horses and even took jumping lessons. He also participated in fox hunts at a local hunt club.

The next several years followed a similar pattern: time spent at Charlottesville teaching, riding horses, and spending time with Jill and her growing family; trips back to Oxford to write and work the farm; occasional visits to other schools like Princeton University, where Faulkner met with students. He seemed to enjoy the routine, and he completed the third book of the Snopes trilogy, *The Mansion*, during this period. His continued horseback riding resulted in several falls and inju-

week, Faulkner refused to go back to the hospital. He took pain medication he had on hand. By July 5, it was clear to Estelle that her husband needed medical care. He was now taking prescription painkillers and washing them down with whiskey. Estelle and Faulkner's nephew Jimmy took him to the hospital.[8]

Once there, the nurses took his pulse and blood pressure, but they appeared normal. When Estelle and Jimmy were sure that he was in capable hands, they left the hospital. About 1:30 a.m. on July 6, Faulkner sat up in his bed, then fell over. He had no pulse. Although a doctor tried to resuscitate him, he could not start Faulkner's heart. The following day, he was buried in St. Peter's Cemetery in Oxford, next to his infant daughter, Alabama.

9 "Boisterous and Enchanting": *The Reivers*

Faulkner's last novel was quite different from his earlier works. Instead of a serious study of guilt and lost traditions, *The Reivers* is a lighthearted story with action and humor. Although the novel was not finished until 1961 and published just before his death, Faulkner first came up with the idea for the book in 1940. At that time, he had described the story in a letter to his editor Robert Haas. "It is a sort of Huck Finn," he said, "a normal boy of about twelve or thirteen, a big, warm-hearted, . . . utterly unreliable white man with the mentality of a child, an old negro family servant, . . . a prostitute not very young . . . and a stolen race horse which none of them actually intended to steal."[1]

The critical response for *The Reivers* was the most positive for any of Faulkner's books in many years. Irving Howe in the *New York Times Book Review* said it was "more easy-spirited and pleasurable than anything Faulkner has written in a long time."[2] William Barrett in *Atlantic Monthly* called it ". . . a boisterous and enchanting comedy from start to finish . . . With *The Reivers* [Faulkner] secures his place among the really superior folk humorists in the American tradition."[3]

Faulkner in 1960, one year before his final novel was published. *The Reivers*, which was not as dark as his previous work, was warmly received by the public and many critics.

Most critics acknowledged that *The Reivers* did not have the depth of the works of Faulkner's earlier years, but they appreciated the humor and folktale qualities of the book. "There is in the book none of the demonic power and little of the dazzling originality of the half dozen great books that appeared from 1929 to 1943," said Granville Hicks in *Saturday Review*, "but there is excitement, and there is humor, and there is a strong moral sense."[4] Barnard Lacy reviewed the book in *Christian Century*. He said: "Here is a great writer enjoying what he is doing—writing a novel with the main purpose of entertaining the reader, and completely succeeding."[5]

A Grandfather's Story

Faulkner establishes the narrative mode of the story with its first two words: "Grandfather said." What follows is the story of eleven-year-old Lucius Priest's adventure in 1905, as told by Lucius to his grandson in about 1960. When Lucius's parents and grandparents take a trip out of town for a funeral, Lucius and his grandfather's driver, Boon Hogganbeck, take Grandfather's car without permission on a trip to visit Miss Corrie, Boon's "girlfriend," a prostitute at Miss Reba's brothel in Memphis. They are too far down the road to turn back when they discover a stowaway, Grandfather's coachman, Ned, hiding under a tarp in the back of the car. The three of them continue to Memphis, where Boon and Lucius go to the brothel (which Boon calls a "boardinghouse") to visit with Miss Corrie, and Ned goes to visit friends.

While at the brothel, Lucius meets Corrie's nephew, a boy about his own age named Otis. Otis is much more world-wise than Lucius and tells him what really goes on at the brothel. Later that evening, Ned reappears with a horse. He has traded Grandfather's car for the horse, and the only way to get the car back is to enter the horse in a race outside of town—and win it. They soon learn that the horse is stolen, but with the help of a railroad flagman (another customer of Miss Corrie's), they are able to put the horse onto a boxcar and get it out of town to the racetrack.

Ned works with the horse, and he teaches Lucius how to ride him. Although the story is complicated by a run-in with a deputy from a nearby town that lands Boon and several of the others in jail, the horse wins the race, and the car is retrieved. Grandfather shows up unexpectedly on the day of the race, and the theft of the car is discovered. By the end of the story, they all go back home, Boon and Miss Corrie get married, and Lucius understands more about what it means to be a man.

Point of View

Unlike other Faulkner stories, this story does not use an omniscient narrator. In this case, the narrator is a character in the book. He tells the story in first-person voice, calling himself "I," and telling it from his own point of view. But this narrator has some advantages over most first-person narrators, who usually tell a story as it happens or soon afterward. Because he is an adult telling the story of his past, the narrator is able to tell us more through his adult eyes than an eleven-year-old would be able to know, and he can share information that he did not find out until later. He is also able to tell us more about the meaning of what he has learned, as he shares with us at the end of the story: "Because now I knew what Grandfather meant: that your outside is just what you live in, sleep in, and has little connection with who you are and even less with what you do."[6]

first-person narrator

A point of view in which the person telling the story is a character in it.

Also unlike most of Faulkner's novels, *The Reivers* stays consistent in one point of view and, except for a flashback with the story of Grandfather's automobile, is told sequentially, without jumping forward and backward in time. The characters are also easier to identify with, and this makes the reader care about what happens to them. According to Lloyd Griffin, who reviewed the book for *Library Journal:* "The story, as other Faulkner tales have not always been, is compelling in all its narrative threads. The author's eye for incident and character is as keen as ever, and his knowledge of both races and of Southern mores is surpassingly impressive."[7]

point of view

The way the author tells a story and the way the reader views it.

As always, Faulkner is skillful at using colloquial or ordinary speech with all his characters. The dialogue of the characters is plain and is true to the patterns of speech of both white and black characters. In one scene, Lucius tells Ned, the black coachman, that Miss Minnie has gone back to Memphis, and Ned talks about their plans to go home: "That's what I figgered. Likely she knows as good as I do it's gonter be a long time before Memphis sees me or Boon Hogganbeck either again. And if Boon's back in jail again, I dont reckon Jefferson, Missippi's gonter see us tonight neither."[8]

The narrative voice of Lucius, the limited point of view, and the colloquial speech of the characters help make *The Reivers* easier reading than many of Faulkner's previous works.

Faulkner's Youth Reflected in *The Reivers*

As Faulkner returns to Yoknapatawpha one last time, he uses familiar characters, like Boon, Ned, and Miss Reba, who have appeared in other stories. At the end, he even introduces the child of Boon and his wife: Lucius Priest Hogganbeck.

As a grandfather himself, Faulkner may have approached the story as Lucius the grandfather did: a way to share a story and pass on the values of his generation to his grandsons. Although the story is fictitious, there are too many similarities between William Faulkner's youth and Lucius Priest to overlook.

Lucius's father, Maury, runs a livery stable, just as Murry Falkner did. Eleven-year-old Lucius has three younger brothers, the youngest still in diapers at the time of the story. Faulkner was also the oldest of four boys, and his brother Dean was only one year old when Faulkner was eleven. Lucius's grandfather is a banker who lives across the street from Lucius's family. Faulkner's grandfather also was a bank president and lived just a few blocks away in Oxford. "Aunt Callie" of *The Reivers* even bears a strong resemblance to "Mammy Callie" of Faulkner's childhood.

Despite these similarities, Faulkner did not enjoy the bond with his own father that Lucius seems to have at the end of the book. Murry Faulkner never acknowledged his son's success as a writer, and he insisted to the end of his life that he had never read any of his son's books or stories.[9] Nor did his father have a good relationship with Faulkner's grandfather. In this way, Faulkner creates a fond vision of a past that was not true in his own youth. Edmond Volpe comments: "It may be that Faulkner enjoyed the irony, as he wrote this final novel, of seeing himself as a grandfather recasting reality, reminiscing about a world that never existed, could never have existed, just as the storytellers of his own youth had created legends of the past."[10]

Racial Issues

For some readers, the comic tone of the book may disguise the more serious issues it treats. Considering the era in which Faulkner wrote the book, when the civil rights movement was just getting started, and Faulkner's willingness to take a public stand on issues relating to race, Faulkner's depiction of the relationship between the races is deliberate. Most of the inequality is based on general assumptions about white and black roles that both races take for granted.

The tone is set at the book's beginning as Boon barges into the livery office to snatch the gun from the desk drawer to shoot a black man (Ludus) who has insulted him. Boon believes this is his God-given right. When he gets the gun, there is little harm done, because Boon is a bad shot and, even with five shots at a man not twenty feet away, he cannot hit him. Ironically, Boon does wound a black girl who is grazed by a bullet. That wound is satisfied with a new dress, a bag of candy, and ten dollars paid to her father.

In this era in the South, most of the people had expectations of propriety about when it is and is not appropriate for whites and blacks to mix. At Miss Ballenbaugh's, Ned is expected to sleep with the blacks, not in the same room with Boon and Lucius. Mr. Binford expects Minnie to serve in the kitchen and sleep in a cot off the storeroom. At the hotel in Parsham, Miss Reba is informed that they have "special quarters for servants, with their own dining room" where Minnie should stay.[11]

Ned plays a significant role in the book. Although he is mostly black and is expected to obey the "rules" for blacks, he is well aware of his blood link to the McCaslin family, and he never lets them forget it. When he introduces himself, he uses a name that identifies him proudly with both the white

The plot of *The Reivers* centers around young Lucius Priest's adventure with his grandfather's driver, Boon Hogganbeck. The novel was turned into a film in 1969, starring Steve McQueen as Boon (left) and Mitch Vogel as Lucius.

McCaslin family and with the place of his birth: Ned William McCaslin Jefferson Mississippi. He is expected to call Boon "Mister," but he often "forgets" to. When Lucius reminds him of it, Ned replies, "I calls him Mister in plenty of time for him to earn it, let alone deserve it."[12]

The real villains of the book are all white. Otis has no redeeming qualities. He is greedy and totally without morals. He is interested only in what will serve his own interest and is willing to lie, cheat, steal, or betray anyone. Butch, the deputy from Hardwick, also is motivated by his own self-interest, most of which concern his lust for Miss Corrie and his desire to win some money in the horse race. Mr. Binford is a minor character in the story, but he, too, is guided by his own interest in the brothel and his vices of drink and gambling. All these characters share a lack of respect for blacks and for women. They violate the code of honor that is a central theme of the book.

Defining Social Codes of the South

Perhaps the most important lesson that Lucius learns through the book is the code of behavior that belongs to a "gentleman." Although Grandfather and others verbalize that code, Lucius already knows most of it, because he was raised in it. He understands it from the beginning of the book, even though he sometimes violates it. In his own way, he educates some of the other characters about the meaning of the word "honor."

An important part of this code is respect for women. Lucius is taught to "make his manners" (bow) to all white women. Miss Reba and Miss Corrie are charmed and flattered. Lucius refuses to drink Mr. Binford's liquor because he has promised his mother that he would never drink unless his father or grandfather invited him. When Mr. Binford points out that Lucius's mother is not present, Lucius still refuses,

Reivers

The Reivers was released as a feature film in 1969. It was nominated for two Academy Awards (John Williams, Best Music; Rupert Crosse, Best Supporting Actor) and won two Golden Globe awards (Steve McQueen, Best Actor; twelve-year-old Mitch Vogel, Best Supporting Actor). In the film, the narrator says, "And so we were three, three reivers high-tailing it for Memphis. Oh, 'reivers'. That's an old-fashioned word from my childhood. In plain English, I'm afraid it meant "thieves."'[13]

because of his promise. When Lucius learns how Otis has degraded Miss Corrie, he jumps to her defense and is injured when Otis swings a knife at him. His action is so significant to Miss Corrie that she decides she will reform in order to be worthy of it. Lucius expects others to follow this code, too. When he finds out that Boon has hit her, he asks, "Why didn't somebody else help her?"[14]

This code of respect extends beyond lines of gender. Grandfather, Lucius's role model of a gentleman, treats everyone with respect: whites, blacks, children, women, prostitutes, even mules. At the end of the book, Grandfather and his "gentleman" friends allow Ned to tell his story, set a chair for him, and offer him a drink. They listen to him, and they trust that he is telling the truth. In return for the respect he gives others, Grandfather receives respect. He is called Boss by family and employees, whether black or white.

Grandfather is certainly not the only gentleman in the book. Mr. Poleymus, the constable in Parsham, is also a gentleman. He cares for his sick wife, he administers justice to both blacks and whites, and he trusts Lucius to the care of

Uncle Parsham. Uncle Parsham, although black, is also a true gentleman. He is wise, kind, gentle, and God-fearing. He has respect for mules as well as for men. He insists that Lucius hear the truth, even when it is unpleasant. All three of these gentlemen teach Lucius an important part of being a man: It is acceptable to cry—but he must wash his face afterward.

Near the end of the book, Grandfather summarizes for Lucius the truth about being a gentleman: "A gentleman can live through anything. He faces anything. A Gentleman accepts the responsibility of his actions and bears the burden of their consequences, even when he did not himself instigate them but only acquiesced to them, didn't say No though he knew he should."[15]

Folk Tales and Legends

The Reivers is told in a style suggestive of legends or tall tales of American folklore. There are no tragic suicides, brutal murders, or executions. Despite the fact that Boon and Lucius spend the night in a brothel, there is little about sex, and even that is shared with the reader in only vague terms. The heroes are good, even when flawed, and the villains are thoroughly bad.

Legends play an important role in the book. As Lucius tells the story, he interjects many other stories that have become legend to the people in Jefferson. We learn the legend of the McCaslins, the Edmondses, and the history of Boon himself. We learn the legend of Miss Ballenbaugh's place with its sordid history of cattle rustling, bootleg whiskey, and gambling. The legend of Ned and the racing mule and even the legend of Grandfather's car all add to the story.

In truth, the story that the grown-up Lucius is telling his grandson is another family legend, a story to be passed down. As in the oral tradition, stories of this kind are meant more to convey tradition and lessons than to be accepted as literal truth. Edmond Volpe sees *The Reivers* as a fairy tale. "The world of the novel is a never-never land where parents are all they should be, prostitutes are reformed by the innocence of a boy, the bad people are thorough-going bogey men, and the rest of the inhabitants may have a few vices, but they are really warm, good-hearted people."[16]

10 Evaluating Faulkner's Work and Legacy

Faulkner is considered among the best American writers of the twentieth century. His work continues to sell and to invite new analysis and interpretation. But even Faulkner is not without critics, and no author's work can be fully discussed without considering both its strengths and weaknesses.

Faulkner's Strengths

Although Faulkner followed others into the literary movement of modernism, he mastered the narrative techniques of the movement in order to enhance his stories. According to Lawrance Thompson of Princeton University, Faulkner refined the techniques that James Joyce and T. S. Eliot introduced in their work. Thompson says that Faulkner's skillful use of stream-of-consciousness narration and nonsequential order of events in the first three sections of *The Sound and the Fury* help to create meaning for the reader, instead of confusion. As each Compson brother tells his piece of the story, Faulkner gives the reader "very striking differences between the personalities of the three brothers; their verbal mannerisms give the artistic illusion that each is unselfconsciously characterizing himself."[1] Thompson's point is that Faulkner

A statue of Faulkner sits in front of City Hall in Oxford, Mississippi. The town has embraced the writer's memory and commemorates the anniversary of his death each year with activities and readings.

did not merely use these techniques to follow the trend; he used them as a masterful way to tell the story most effectively.

Faulkner also used allusions to myth and symbolism as ways to add meaning to his stories. As literature professor Edmond Volpe says, "Faulkner's greatness as an artist is due to a great extent to what might be called his stereoscopic vision, his ability to deal with the specific and the universal simultaneously, to make the real symbolic without sacrificing reality."[2] In most of Faulkner's stories, the characters' struggles are those of all people: the quest for power, for love, for knowledge, for dignity, or just for survival.

The culture of the American South is so significant in Faulkner's works that it becomes the lens through which the reader sees the story. His stories explore the attitudes of plantation owners and slaves, aristocrats and peasants, town dwellers and farmers. Whether a story takes place before, during, or after the Civil War, the roles of and the rules for whites, blacks, men, and women are dictated by the culture of slavery and the traditional values of the antebellum South. Literary critic Michael Millgate says that "for Faulkner, as a Southerner intensely aware of the past of his own region and of his own family, the South was not merely an obvious subject for his fiction but fiercely and inescapably, the inevitable subject."[3]

But despite Faulkner's identification with this culture that he knows so well, the basic truths of his stories are not limited by geography. Critic Mary Cooper Robb says: "Actually, Yoknapatawpha County has its counterparts all over the world, wherever there are people who live by the land and live poorly, whose past is greater than their present, and who have the problem of an alien race to whom justice must be done."[4] Likewise, Robert Penn Warren said that Faulkner's works should be understood "in terms of issues which are common to our modern world. The legend is not merely a legend of the South, but is also a legend of our general plight and problem."[5]

Faulkner's Weaknesses

Although Faulkner's work has been widely respected for many years, some critics point out areas where they believe Faulkner fails. Interestingly, some of these weaknesses are closely tied to the acknowledged strengths of his work. Despite the effectiveness of some of his narrative techniques, many readers find the vocabulary and sentence structure of the writing difficult to understand. Malcolm Cowley commented, "Two or three of his books as a whole and many of them in part are awkward experiments. All of them are full of overblown words . . . that he would have used with more discretion, or not at all, if he had . . . served an apprenticeship to an older writer."[6]

While myth and allusion are used well in most of the works, occasionally Faulkner sacrificed the realism of a story for the sake of the symbolism. *A Fable*, with its direct allusion to the story of Christ, is generally considered among the weakest of Faulkner's books. Despite the fact that it won both a Pulitzer Prize and the National Book Award, it has generally been ignored by critics. Most, like Lawrance Thompson, consider the allegory too forced. Thompson praises most of Faulkner's work for its mixture of realism and symbolism, but he says that "*A Fable* fails, as a work of narrative art, partly because Faulkner there lost the balance between the two modes."[7]

Even Faulkner's portrayal of the South is a source of disagreement among critics. Some object to Faulkner's portrayal of the respectful and generous slaveholder/employer and the patient and contented slave/servant. They believe that Faulkner and his characters are nostalgic for a tradition that never existed—that the Southern gentleman was never a real gentleman at all. English professor Christopher C. De Santis calls the author's depiction of the Reconstruction era (the years after the Civil War) "pseudo-history" and a reflection of Faulkner's own prejudices.[8]

realism

In a story, showing life as it really is, both good and bad.

Few female characters in Faulkner's fiction are allowed to display morality, strength, independence, or intelligence. While there are kind mothers and mother figures (many of them African American servants), most younger women are portrayed as sex objects. Literary critic Mary Cooper Robb said that Faulkner "never seems to make a reality of women unless they are what has been called 'Southern madonnas of low mentality' or stubbornly old and tough." She adds that the younger women in his work are often "Faulknerian versions of the flapper, skinny, brainless, and oversexed."[9]

Some readers find Faulkner's works too pessimistic. They believe that the violence, cruelty, immorality, and despair of the characters makes the reading unrewarding. "There is a tragic note in Faulkner's famous tortured prose," said Harold C. Gardiner, "an overtone that he perhaps never intended or even recognized. It is a reverberation of regret that Faulkner's characters never realize the full nobility of the values for which they fought."[10] Warwick Wadlington agrees. "Experiences often come to Faulkner's people too early or too late, leaving wounds or nostalgia; they are over too quickly to be appreciated, leaving regrets; they are too slippery or ambiguous to be grasped, leaving confusion."[11]

On the contrary, Mary Cooper Robb says that this unpleasantness is necessary in order for the author to succeed:

Faulkner's former home is now a museum and literary destination for his many fans. Here, visitors gather on the lawn of Rowan Oak in 2006 to hear a reading of "A Rose for Emily."

In a sense he is deeply conscious of evil, but in a more positive way than the critics imply. His primary concern, after all, is to show that a man must choose between right and wrong, for one set of human values and against another. The choosing must inevitably involve conflict, which, indeed, is one of the necessary ingredients of any story . . . To tell a story of courage the writer must also make clear the possibility of abject fear. If he writes of honor, he must also write of dishonor . . . Failing to show or to make implicit these opposites the writer also fails to impart to his readers the intensity of experience they are seeking.[12]

Soon after Faulkner's death in 1962, an article in *Newsweek* considered this range of critical opinion: "What do critics make of him? Surveying them in mass and letting their contradictions cancel each other out, they seem to establish only one thing—that Faulkner, like a few great writers of the past, has created a world and that he has cast across it the brooding shadow of his own extraordinary soul."[13]

Faulkner's Influence and Legacy

Many literary critics and scholars have posed the question: "What has Faulkner left us?" Certainly, his nineteen novels and dozens of short stories are a legacy in themselves. But Faulkner has left much more for us than just reading material.

Faulkner's Film Legacy

When considering the work of Faulkner's career, we sometimes forget that a substantial portion of his legacy was never published for the reading public. Faulkner's work for Hollywood included six major motion pictures for which he received credit and another ten on which he collaborated but was not listed in the films' credits. Among his credited films are *To Have and Have Not, The Big Sleep,* and *The Road to Glory.* Among his uncredited films are *Mildred Pierce, Gunga Din,* and *God Is My Co-Pilot.* His films featured some of the top actors of the era: Humphrey Bogart, Errol Flynn, Joan Crawford, and many more. Now, more than fifty years after his death, many of these films are considered classics. In 1964 poet and novelist George Garrett commented, "Of all our major novelists, William Faulkner has been the most successful as a screenwriter, as fact that is not without honor and one which certainly cannot be safely ignored by the critics."[14]

Influence of Technique

Faulkner challenged the boundaries of narrative style by using shifting narrators, non-chronological plots, stream-of-consciousness narration, narration by characters who are mentally disabled, and characters who play roles in different stories. In doing so, he broke free of the traditions of novel-writing that had existed before. English professor Philip Weinstein contends that Faulkner's breakthrough as a creative writer came when he realized that the conventions of storytelling could be altered.[15] These techniques that Faulkner pioneered have given later writers more freedom in choosing their styles of storytelling.

A recent book by Margaret Donovan Bauer identifies many authors whose work has shown the influence of Faulkner. She names some writers from Faulkner's era, such as Zora Neale Hurston and Ellen Glasgow, whose writings explore similar issues to Faulkner's but from different perspectives. Bauer also describes the work of contemporary writers like Larry McMurtry (the Pulitzer Prize–winning author of *Lonesome Dove*) and others whose works she says "echo Faulkner without reservation. They recast his plots and themes but continue to pursue the issues and examine the characters that intrigued this apparent mentor."[16]

A Voice for the South

One of the most striking qualities of Faulkner's work is the importance of the culture of the rural South. It is a culture separate and distinctly different from other regions of the United States, and one that is steeped in history. But it had seldom had a voice like Faulkner's. George Garrett points out, "The southern writer is very much aware that Faulkner did not invent his material. It was there to be mined and explored."[17]

Southern authors of Faulkner's era and those who came later always faced the comparison of their work to his. Faulkner's enormous reputation carried power, like that of a locomotive, to mow down anything in its path. Author Flannery O'Connor once said, "The presence alone of Faulkner in our midst makes a great difference in what the writer can and cannot permit himself to do. Nobody wants his mule and wagon stalled on the same track the Dixie Limited is roaring down."[18]

Despite this risk, other writers from the South and elsewhere have been influenced by Faulkner and have adopted similar techniques and themes in their work. American Indian author Louise Erdrich's novel *Tracks* has been compared with *Absalom, Absalom!*, and Toni Morrison's *Song of Solomon* has been compared to *Go Down, Moses*, *Absalom, Absalom!*, and *The Sound and the Fury*. In an article in *The Mississippi Quarterly*, Lorie Watkins Fulton says, "Morrison, consciously or unconsciously, reprises Faulkner's original theme and makes it her own in this novel that celebrates community and vanquishes the destructive isolation that she sees as the dark heart of Faulkner's fiction.[19]

Race in Faulkner

Another recurrent element in Faulkner's writing is the issue of racism. In Faulkner's time before the civil rights movement, prejudice and discrimination were still very much a part of life in the South. Faulkner confronted the issue directly, delving into the generations of his characters to explore the history of slavery in their past and how it affected succeeding generations. Weinstein says, "He took the measure of what it cost whites to have to hate blacks, as well as the cost that blacks—sometimes not knowing they were black—had to pay."[20]

While we would wish that it weren't so, racism is still very much an issue in America, and therefore Faulkner's work is as relevant in this area as ever. Speaking of the issue in Faulkner's *Absalom! Absalom!*, John Jeremiah Sullivan says, "Racism is still our madness. The longer that remains the case, the more vital this book grows, for Faulkner is one of the great explorers of this madness."[21]

Universal Themes

In his Nobel Prize acceptance speech in 1950, Faulkner spoke of the writer's duty to write about man's "spirit capable of compassion and sacrifice and endurance," and "his privilege to help man endure by lifting his heart, by reminding him of the courage and honor and hope and pride and compassion and pity and sacrifice which have been the glory of his past."[22]

Fifty years after Faulkner's death, Weinstein asked, "Do his novels still live in 2013? and if they do, what in them still burns fiercely, still has the power to astonish his readers?"[23] The answer to that question may be this comment from a Faulkner scholar: "Faulkner's universal themes are relative to the same human emotional expression across centuries, generations, and the relationships within them."[24]

While Faulkner's stories are firmly rooted in the South, they address universal themes that extend far beyond geographical boundaries.

Faulkner in the Digital Age

Despite the passage of time, Faulkner's work has retained its relevance to readers today. But, in this age of digital media and instantaneous communication, the complexity of Faulkner's work can try our patience. The question for many readers in the twenty-first century may be, "Why bother?" What is there in Faulkner's work that makes it worth the effort?

In an essay published by the Center for Faulkner Studies, a college professor was asked this same question. He explained that the very complexity of Faulkner's work is one of the most important reasons for students and other readers to accept the challenge: "His work demands close reading and deep thinking—crucial skills for students, given the shorter information bursts they read on technology today."[25]

But even Faulkner has a presence in the digital age: his own Facebook author page. Faulkner's photo is there, with a picture of Rowan Oak as the cover photo. Posts on the page highlight theater productions, book covers, quotations from the author, etc. Over three hundred thousand followers testify to Faulkner's continuing appeal to readers in the twenty-first century.

Chronology

1897– William Falkner is born in New Albany, Mississippi.

1905– Murry and Maud Falkner move to Oxford, Mississippi, with William and his two younger brothers, Murry and John.

1907– Brother Dean is born.

1915– William drops out of school during his second attempt at eleventh grade.

1918– Falkner is rejected by the US military; changes spelling of name to Faulkner; joins Canadian Royal Air Force and begins training; discharged in December after World War I ends.

1919– Poem "L'Après-Midi d'un Faune" is published in *New Republic*; Faulkner enrolls at University of Mississippi.

1924– Pays to have *The Marble Faun*, a collection of his poems, published.

1926– First novel, *Soldiers' Pay,* is published.

1929– Marries Estelle Franklin; *Sartoris* and *The Sound and the Fury* are published.

1930– "A Rose for Emily," his first short story for a national magazine, is published; *As I Lay Dying* is published.

1931– Daughter Alabama is born but lives only nine days; *Sanctuary* and *These 13* published.

1932– Accepts first contract with MGM, beginning a career as a screenwriter; *Light in August* is published.

1933– Daughter Jill is born.

1935– Youngest brother, Dean Faulkner, is killed in crash of the plane he bought from William; *Pylon* published.

1936-1946– Published novels include *Absalom, Absalom!*, *The Unvanquished*, *The Wild Palms*, *The Hamlet*, and *Go Down, Moses*. Faulkner is elected to National Institute of Arts and Letters in 1939.

1948-1951– Elected to American Academy of Arts and Letters; awarded Medal for Fiction by American Academy of Arts and Letters and Nobel Prize in Literature.

1954-1955– *A Fable* is published; it wins both the National Book Award and the Pulitzer Prize.

1956– Begins work at University of Virginia as writer-in-residence.

1957-1959– Finishes the Snopes trilogy with *The Town* and *The Mansion*.

1962– Awarded Gold Medal for Fiction by the National Institute of Arts and Letters; *The Reivers* is published; injured in fall from a horse on June 17 and dies of heart failure on July 6.

1968– Rowan Oak is declared a National Historic Landmark

1972– Estelle Faulkner passes away on May 11 in Oxford. Jill Faulkner Summers sells Rowan Oak to the University of Mississippi.

1981– The first annual PEN/Faulkner Awards for Fiction are awarded to the year's best fiction works by living American authors.

1989– The Center for Faulkner Studies is established at Southeast Missouri State University in Cape Girardeau, Missouri, devoted to the study and teaching of Faulkner.

Chapter Notes

Chapter 1. William Faulkner's Small World

1. "William Faulkner: Faith That Man Will Prevail," *Newsweek*, July 16, 1962, 52.
2. *National Review*, July 31, 1962, 54.
3. Joseph Blotner, *Faulkner: A Biography* (New York: Random House, 1974), vol. I, vii.
4. Mary Cooper Robb, *William Faulkner: An Estimate of His Contribution to the Modern American Novel* (Pittsburgh: University of Pittsburgh Press, 1963), 16.
5. Edmond Volpe, *A Reader's Guide to William Faulkner: The Novels* (Syracuse, NY: Syracuse University Press, 2003), 32.
6. Robb, 8.
7. Volpe, 23.
8. Ibid., 31–32.

Chapter 2. The Young Writer

1. Joseph Blotner, *Faulkner: A Biography* (New York: Random House, 1974), vol. I, vii.
2. David Minter, *William Faulkner: His Life and Works* (Baltimore, MD: Johns Hopkins University Press, 1980), 8.
3. Blotner, 105.
4. Ibid., 110–111.
5. Minter, 12.
6. Ibid., 27.
7. Blotner, 228.
8. Michel Gresset, *A Faulkner Chronology* (Jackson, MS: University Press of Mississippi, 1985), 17.
9. Ibid., 20.
10. Blotner, 505.
11. Minter, 54.

12. Martin Kreiswirth, *William Faulkner: The Making of a Novelist* (Athens, GA: University of Georgia Press, 1983), 112.
13. Gresset, 26.
14. Blotner, 560.
15. Kreiswirth, 110.
16. Blotner, 562.
17. Minter, 81.
18. Marion Knight, Mertice James, and Ruth Lechlitner, eds., *Book Review Digest* (New York: H. W. Wilson Co., 1930), 302.

Chapter 3. Faulkner's Breakthrough: *The Sound and the Fury*

1. Marion Knight, Mertice James, and Ruth Lechlitner, eds., *Book Review Digest* (New York: H. W. Wilson Co., 1930), 303.
2. Ibid.
3. Cheryl Lester, "*The Sound and the Fury* and the Great Migration," in Philip M. Weinstein, ed., *The Cambridge Companion to William Faulkner* (Cambridge, England: Cambridge University Press, 1995), 123.
4. James B. Meriwether and Michael Millgate, *Lion in the Garden: Interviews With William Faulkner, 1926–1962* (New York: Random House, 1968), 222.
5. Ibid., 92.
6. William Faulkner, *The Sound and the Fury* (New York: Modern Library/Random House, 1946), 6.
7. Meriwether and Millgate, 146.
8. Faulkner, 16.
9. Ibid., 313.
10. William Shakespeare, *Macbeth*, Act V, Scene 5.

11. Meriwether and Millgate, 245.
12. Faulkner, 55.
13. Ibid., 261.
14. Perrin Lowry, "Concepts of Time in *The Sound and the Fury*," in Michael H. Cowan, ed., *Twentieth Century Interpretations of* The Sound and the Fury (Englewood Cliffs, NJ: Prentice-Hall, 1968), 59.
15. Faulkner, 57–58.
16. Ibid., 290.
17. Olga W. Vickery, "Worlds in Counterpoint," in Michael H. Cowan, ed., *Twentieth Century Interpretations of* The Sound and the Fury (Englewood Cliffs, NJ: Prentice-Hall, 1968), 41.
18. Edmond Volpe, *A Reader's Guide to William Faulkner* (Syracuse, NY: Syracuse University Press, 2003), 126.
19. Ibid.

Chapter 4. Triumph and Trouble

1. David Minter, *William Faulkner: His Life and Works* (Baltimore, MD: Johns Hopkins University Press, 1980), 110.
2. Joseph Blotner, *Faulkner: A Biography* (New York: Random House, 1974), vol. I, 634.
3. James B. Meriwether and Michael Millgate, *Lion in the Garden: Interviews With William Faulkner, 1926–1962* (New York: Random House, 1968), 222.
4. Ibid., 180.
5. Meriwether and Millgate, 123.
6. Jay Parini, *One Matchless Time: A Life of William Faulkner* (New York: Harper Collins, 2004), 156.
7. Blotner, 687.
8. Ibid., 685.

9. Minter, 133.
10. Michel Gresset, *A Faulkner Chronology* (Jackson, MS: University Press of Mississippi, 1985), 42.
11. "The Story of Temple Drake (1933). Trivia," *IMDb*, accessed July 2, 2015, http://www.imdb.com/title/tt0024617/trivia?ref_=tt_ql_2.
12. William Faulkner, Letter to Joan Williams, August 8, 1952, in Joseph Blotner, ed., *Selected Letters of William Faulkner* (New York: Random House, 1977), 338.
13. Parini, 279.

Chapter 5. Examining Three Short Stories

1. Michel Gresset, *A Faulkner Chronology* (Jackson, MS: University Press of Mississippi, 1985), 29–31.
2. Hans H. Skei, *William Faulkner: The Short Story Career* (Oslo, Norway: Universitetsforlaget, 1981), 14.
3. Edmond Volpe, *A Reader's Guide to William Faulkner: The Novels* (Syracuse, NY: Syracuse University Press, 2003), 29.
4. William Faulkner, *Collected Stories of William Faulkner* (New York: Random House, 1934), 119–120.
5. Ibid., 130.
6. Ibid., 123.
7. Ibid., 126.
8. James B. Meriwether and Michael Millgate, *Lion in the Garden: Interviews With William Faulkner, 1926–1962* (New York: Random House, 1968), 127.
9. Edmond Volpe, *A Reader's Guide to William Faulkner: The Short Stories* (Syracuse, NY: Syracuse University Press, 2004), 99.
10. Ibid., 104.

11. William Faulkner, Letter to Roberts Haas, December 15, 1938, in Joseph Blotner, ed., *Selected Letters of William Faulkner* (New York: Random House, 1977), 108.
12. Skei, 93.
13. Faulkner, *Collected Stories of William Faulkner*, 8.
14. Ibid., 21.
15. Ibid., 3.
16. Ibid., 11.
17. Ibid., 10.
18. Ibid., 11.
19. Ibid.
20. Volpe, *A Reader's Guide to William Faulkner: The Short Stories*, 236.
21. Ibid., 236–238.
22. Michael Millgate, "The Unity of *Go Down, Moses*," in Francis Lee Utley, Lynn Z. Bloom, and Arthur F. Kinney, eds., *Bear, Man, and God* (New York: Random House, 1971), 224.
23. John Faulkner, excerpt from *My Brother Bill*, in Utley, Bloom, and Kinney, 96.
24. Quoted by Millgate, 224.
25. Ron Rash, "Do You Write, Mr. Faulkner?" *Sporting Classics Daily*, November 20, 2014, http://sportingclassicsdaily.com/issue/2015-1/article/do-you-write-mr-faulkner.
26. William Faulkner, *Go Down, Moses* (New York: Random House/Modern Library, 1942), 331.
27. Faulkner, *Go Down, Moses*, 192.
28. Ibid., 237.
29. Ibid., 328.
30. Ibid., 257.
31. Ibid., 321.
32. Ibid., 250.

33. Volpe, *A Reader's Guide to William Faulkner: The Novels*, 243.

Chapter 6. The Struggling Writer

1. David Minter, *William Faulkner: His Life and Works* (Baltimore, MD: Johns Hopkins University Press, 1980), 178.
2. Joseph Blotner, *Faulkner: A Biography* (New York: Random House, 1974), II, 1042.
3. "*The Big Sleep* (1946). Trivia," *IMDb*, http://www.imdb.com/title/tt0038355/trivia?ref_=tt_ql_2 (accessed July 2, 2015).
4. William Faulkner, Letter to Harold Ober, January 5, 1946, in Joseph Blotner, ed., *Selected Letters of William Faulkner* (New York: Random House, 1977), 217–218.
5. Jay Parini, *One Matchless Time: A Life of William Faulkner* (New York: Harper Collins, 2004), 301.
6. Blotner, 1257.
7. Parini, 329.
8. William Faulkner, "Address Upon Receiving the Nobel Prize for Literature," in James B. Meriwether, ed., *Essays, Speeches, & Public Letters* (New York: Random House, 1965), 120.
9. Michel Gresset, *A Faulkner Chronology* (Jackson, MS: University Press of Mississippi, 1985), 89.
10. Blotner, 1466.
11. James B. Meriwether and Michael Millgate, *Lion in the Garden: Interviews With William Faulkner, 1926–1962* (New York: Random House, 1968), 226.

Chapter 7. Controversial Masterpiece: *A Fable*

1. Jay Parini, *One Matchless Time: A Life of William Faulkner* (New York: Harper Collins, 2004), 365.

2. Mertice James and Dorothy Brown, eds., *The Book Review Digest, 1954* (New York: H. W. Wilson Co., 1955), 298.
3. Charles J. Rolo, "Reader's Choice," *Atlantic Monthly*, September 1954, 79–80.
4. Herbert Cahoon, *Library Journal*, August 1954, 1400.
5. William Faulkner, *A Fable* (New York: Random House, 1954), 437.
6. James and Brown, 298.
7. Riley Hughes, "Novels Reviewed by Riley Hughes," *Catholic World*, November 1954, 150.
8. James B. Meriwether and Michael Millgate, *Lion in the Garden: Interviews With William Faulkner, 1926–1962* (New York: Random House, 1968), 113.
9. Ibid., 247.
10. Ibid.
11. Faulkner, 54.
12. Hughes, 150.
13. Edmond Volpe, *A Reader's Guide to William Faulkner: The Novels* (Syracuse, NY: Syracuse University Press, 2003), 287.
14. Faulkner, 203.
15. Meriwether and Millgate, 113.
16. James and Brown, 299.

Chapter 8. Faulkner's Last Years

1. Jay Parini, *One Matchless Time: A Life of William Faulkner* (New York: Harper Collins, 2004), 356–357.
2. Ibid., 367–368.
3. "Guidelines for Handling William Faulkner's Drinking During Foreign Trips From the US State Department (1955)," *Open Culture*, February 27, 2015, http://www.

openculture.com/2015/02/guidelines-for-handling-william-faulkners-drinking.htm.

4. Joseph Blotner, *Faulkner: A Biography* (New York, Random House, 1974), vol. II, 1533.
5. William Faulkner, Letter to Else Jonsson, June 12, 1955, in Joseph Blotner, ed., *Selected Letters of William Faulkner* (New York: Random House, 1977), 382.
6. William Faulkner, "A Letter to the Leaders of the Negro Race" [originally published as "If I Were a Negro"], in James B. Meriwether, ed., *Essays, Speeches, & Public Letters* (New York: Random House, 1965), 111.
7. Blotner, 1821.
8. Ibid., 1835–1836.

Chapter 9. "Boisterous and Enchanting": *The Reivers*

1. William Faulkner, Letter to Robert Haas, May 3, 1940, in Joseph Blotner, ed., *Selected Letters of William Faulkner* (New York: Random House, 1977), 123.
2. Dorothy P. Davison, *The Book Review Digest, 1962* (New York: H. W. Wilson, 1963), 372.
3. William Barrett, "Reader's Choice," *Atlantic Monthly*, July 1962, 109–110.
4. Granville Hicks, "Building Blocks of a Gentleman," *Saturday Review*, June 2, 1962, 27.
5. Bernard Lacy, "Felicitous Finale," *Christian Century*, September 19, 1962, 1136.
6. William Faulkner, *The Reivers: A Reminiscence* (New York: Random House, 1962), 304.
7. Lloyd W. Griffin, *Library Journal*, June 1, 1962, 2156.
8. Faulkner, *The Reivers*, 283.

9. David Minter, *William Faulkner: His Life and Works* (Baltimore, MD: Johns Hopkins University Press, 1980), 16.
10. Edmond Volpe, *A Reader's Guide to William Faulkner: The Novels* (Syracuse, NY: Syracuse University Press, 2003), 349.
11. Faulkner, *The Reivers*, 199.
12. Ibid., 55.
13. "*The Reivers* (1969)," *IMDb*, http://www.imdb.com/title/tt0038355/trivia?ref_=tt_ql_2 (accessed July 3, 2015).
14. Faulkner, *The Reivers*, 256.
15. Ibid, 302.
16. Volpe, 345.

Chapter 10. Evaluating Faulkner's Work and Legacy

1. Lawrance Thompson, *William Faulkner: An Introduction and Interpretation* (New York: Barnes and Noble, 1963), 20.
2. Edmond Volpe, *A Reader's Guide to William Faulkner: The Novels* (Syracuse, NY: Syracuse University Press, 2003), 28.
3. Michael Millgate, *William Faulkner* (New York: Capricorn Books, 1961), 4.
4. Mary Cooper Robb, *William Faulkner: An Estimation of His Contribution to the Modern American Novel* (Pittsburgh: University of Pittsburgh Press, 1963), 16.
5. Millgate, 108.
6. "The Writer in Critical Perspective," *Saturday Review*, July 28, 1962, 22.
7. Thompson, 27.
8. Christopher C. De Santis, "Pseudo-History Versus Social Critique: Faulkner's Reconstruction," *Southern Quarterly*, Fall 2005, 9–10.
9. Robb, 41.

10. Harold C. Gardiner, "Recalling Faulkner," *America*, July 21, 1962, 519.
11. Warwick Wadlington, "Reading Faulkner" in Philip M. Weinstein, ed., *The Cambridge Companion to William Faulkner* (Cambridge, England: Cambridge University Press, 1995), 207.
12. Robb, 24.
13. "William Faulkner: Faith That Man Will Prevail," 53.
14. George Garrett, "The Influence of William Faulkner," *Georgia Review* 18, no. 4 (Winter 1964): 419-427.
15. Philip Weinstein, "He Made the Books and He Died: The Fiftieth Anniversary of Faulkner's Death," *Sewanee Review* 121, no. 3 (2013): 435.
16. Margaret Donovan Bauer, *William Faulkner's Legacy: "What Shadow, What Stain, What Mark"* (Gainesville, FL: University Press of Florida, 2005), 2.
17. Garrett, 420.
18. Flannery O'Connor, "Some Aspects of the Grotesque in Southern Fiction" in Sally and Robert Fitzgerald, eds., *Mystery and Manners* (New York: Farrar, Straus, & Giroux, 1962), 45.
19. Lorie Watkins Fulton, "William Faulkner Reprised: Isolation in Toni Morrison's Song of Solomon," *Mississippi Quarterly*, Winter 2004/2005, 10.
20. Weinstein, 436.
21. John Jeremiah Sullivan, "How William Faulkner Tackled Race—And Freed the South From Itself," *New York Times Magazine*, http://www.nytimes.com/2012/07/01/magazine/how-william-faulkner-tackled-race-and-freed-the-south-from-itself.html?_r=1.
22. William Faulkner, "Address upon Receiving the Nobel Prize for Literature," in James B. Meriwether, ed., *Essays,*

Speeches, & Public Letters (New York: Random House, 1965), 120.
23. Weinstein, 433.
24. "Why Faulkner, Still?" Center for Faulkner Studies, Southeast Missouri State University, http://www.semo.edu/cfs/teaching/34289.html. (accessed June 28, 2015).
25. Ibid.

Literary Terms

allegory—A story that symbolically suggests a deeper meaning.

allusion—Referring to a character, setting, or other elements of a famous story to suggest a similarity.

colloquial—Everyday speech that is informal and might be used in casual conversation.

first-person narrator—A point of view in which the person telling the story is a character in it.

flashback—A story inside a story that tells about something that happened before the main story.

imagery—Use of sensory details; how things, look, smell, feel, sound, or taste.

jargon—Specialized language or terms related to a particular activity, career area, or field that people outside that field might not be familiar with.

modernism—Literary style that originated after World War I. Techniques of modernism include use of stream-of-consciousness narration, application of psychological theory to characters, and events that are not in chronological order.

motif—An object or element that appears frequently throughout a work of literature.

myth—Classical story, passed down through the oral tradition, such as Greek mythology or other traditional story that is usually accepted as fictional.

omniscient narrator—A voice telling the story that is all-knowing.

plot—The events of the story; what happens.

point of view—The way the author tells a story, and the way the reader views it.

protagonist—Main character in a story, usually the one through which readers experience the story.

realism—In a story, showing life as it really is, both good and bad.

stream of consciousness—Style of narration in which the story is told through a character's thoughts as he or she experiences the events.

symbolism—Using one element in a story to stand for something else.

theme—A message about human behavior or about life or society that a writer may suggest.

Major Works by William Faulkner

Novels

Soldiers' Pay (1926)
Mosquitoes (1927)
Sartoris (1929)
The Sound and the Fury (1929)
As I Lay Dying (1930)
Sanctuary (1931)
Light in August (1932)
Pylon (1935)
Absalom, Absalom! (1936)
The Unvanquished (1938)
The Wild Palms (1939)
The Hamlet (1940)
Go Down, Moses and Other Stories (1942)
Intruder in the Dust (1948)
Requiem for a Nun (1951)
A Fable (1954)
The Town (1957)
The Mansion (1959)
The Reivers (1962)

Short Story Collections

These 13 (1931)
Doctor Martino and Other Stories (1934)
The Portable Faulkner (1946)
Knight's Gambit (1949)
Collected Stories (1950)
The Faulkner Reader: Selections From the Works of William Faulkner (1954)

Faulkner's County: Tales of Yoknapatawpha County (1955)
Big Woods (1955)
Uncle Willy, and Other Stories (1958)
Selected Short Stories (1961)

Lectures, Speeches, and Other Writings

Faulkner at Nagano, edited by Robert A. Jelliffe (1956)
Faulkner in the University: Class Conferences at the University of Virginia 1957–1958, edited by Frederick L. Gwynn and Joseph L. Blotner (1959)
William Faulkner: Early Prose and Poetry, edited by Carvel Collins (1962)
Essays, Speeches, and Public Letters, edited by James B. Meriwether (1966).
Lion in the Garden: Interviews With William Faulkner 1926–1962, edited by James B. Meriwether and Michael Millgate (1968)
Selected Letters of William Faulkner, edited by Joseph Blotner (1977)

Further Reading

Fargnoli, A. Nicholas, and Michael Golay. *William Faulkner A to Z: The Essential Reference to His Life and Work*. New York: Facts on File, 2002.

Faulkner, Jim. *Across the Creek: Faulkner Family Stories.* Jackson, MS: University Press of Mississippi, 2006.

Johnson, Claudia Durst. *Family Dysfunction in William Faulkner's As I Lay Dying*. San Diego: Greenhaven, 2013.

Porter, Carolyn. *William Faulkner.* New York: Oxford University Press, 2007.

Trefzer, Annette, and Ann J. Abadie, eds. *Faulkner and Mystery.* Jackson, MS: University Press of Mississippi, 2014.

Internet Addresses

William Faulkner on the Web

www.mcsr.olemiss.edu/~egjbp/faulkner/faulkner.html

Includes many resources about Faulkner, his life, his writing, his movies, his hometown, and more.

Faulkner at Virginia

faulkner.lib.virginia.edu

Provides specific information about Faulkner's work at the University of Virginia, including audio files of some of the lectures and speeches he gave there.

Rowan Oak

www.rowanoak.com

Faulkner's home for over thirty years is open to the public as a museum. The website tells about the home and includes video and photos.

Mississippi Writers' Page

www.olemiss.edu/mwp/dir/faulkner_william/

Includes biography, photos, and links to scholarly books about Faulkner. You can also learn about many other Mississippi writers by clicking the "authors" link under the page heading.

INDEX